How
To
Feel
Good
About Yourself

12 Key Steps To
Positive Self-Esteem

I'm not OK, you're not OK—and that's OK.
                                        —William Sloane Coffin

How
To
Feel
Good
About Yourself

12 Key Steps To
Positive Self-Esteem

Christopher Ebbe, Ph.D., ABPP

Christopher Ebbe, Ph.D.
943 Scripps Dr.
Claremont CA 91711

ISBN: 978-0-615-24647-5
Printed in the United States of America

Previously published by
Wellness Institute, Gretna LA
(ISBN: 1-58741-1113)

Cover design by Wellness Institute
Copy editing by Shaundra Sumpter

This book is dedicated to my loving wife and partner in all things, Patricia, from whom I have learned so much about love and self-esteem.

Table of Contents

PREFACE

This book is about self-esteem—one of the issues most relevant to our emotional health. Poor self-esteem causes an amazing amount of emotional pain and unhappiness and is surprisingly widespread. All of us need positive self-esteem if we are to function well in the world. The enormous cost of poor self-esteem for a large number of people in our society, in terms of impaired effectiveness and productivity, as well as emotional pain, goes largely unrecognized, because most people with poor self-esteem believe that they deserve to feel that way and because our culture itself in some ways approves of manipulating self-esteem as a means of keeping people from demanding societal changes and a means of inducing people to consume more and more goods and services. All of us have shortcomings and problems. Nobody is perfect. The fact of the matter is that I'm not OK, you're not OK, and yet that's OK! At its simplest, positive self-esteem is just accepting ourselves. Even if we strive to be better, at the end of every day we need to feel good about ourselves.

We will provide definitions and concepts to make self-esteem understandable and then discuss strategies for improving self-esteem that will involve (1) changing our own definitions of ourselves (how we view and understand ourselves); (2) taking primary charge of our perceptions and feelings about ourselves and our identities (instead of allowing others to determine how we define ourselves and how we perceive and feel about ourselves); (3) improving our relationship with ourselves; (4) dealing with others who may wish (consciously or unconsciously) to keep us feeling bad about ourselves for their own advantage; and (5) dealing with the influences on us of our culture and the ways in which it manipulates self-esteem.

This book does not propose easy or quick solutions to the problem of poor self-esteem. Your self-esteem stems from basic attitudes and assumptions you have about yourself, and these must change if your self-esteem is to improve. This book presents a "philosophy of self-esteem"—a set of beliefs and attitudes and their expressions in behavior, which is designed to help you to be the kind of person who naturally has good self-esteem.

Efforts to be "better than" others are generally attempts to compensate for poor self-esteem. For many people, striving to look beautiful, win, achieve status or position, or acquire possessions is often a sad or even desperate attempt to make up for feeling bad about oneself.

You will almost certainly try to avoid or pull back from doing what is necessary to improve your self-esteem (even though you say that you want better self-esteem), and serious self-exploration and facing up to your inner pain will be necessary in order to feel better about yourself. The book will support you in this process.

Everyone deserves the chance to have good self-esteem, and those who act in ways that prevent this, such as parents who try to make their children feel as if they are "bad" and citizens who look down on those of another race or religion, are actually actively harming others while they exercise their right to free thought or free speech. This may give us pause to reconsider the relative merits of these rights!

Self-esteem and how you relate to yourself form one of the essential cornerstones of emotional health in general (along with perceiving and understanding things accurately and being able to relate to others effectively). Pursuing the ideas in this book will improve your emotional health in general, how you feel every day, and your ability to relate to others.

While the ideas presented here have not all been verified by psychological research, they are all widely accepted in clinical work. The amount of benefit for you of applying this system will depend mostly on your willingness and desire to change, the persistence and good judgment with which you apply the principles in your life, and your current self-esteem and life situation. It will be reasonably safe to implement these ideas in your life if you do so with reasonably good judgment and common sense.

Every philosophical or therapeutic system has goals in terms of the kind of people or the kind of life it wishes to produce. The choice of principles here is aimed at producing loving, cooperative, self-aware, self-confident, empathic, and compassionate people. This describes a way of being and an existence that has the greatest chance of maximizing fulfillment, contentment, and satisfaction, and of minimizing conflict, hatred, and violence.

There are inevitably some risks to changing your beliefs and behavior, such as becoming dissatisfied with previous relationships and not liking the truths that you discover about those around you when you learn to view them more realistically.

Some fear that increased self-esteem will make people more selfish and less responsive to their fellow men and to their responsibilities. Nothing could be further from the concept of healthy and responsible self-esteem. In order to succeed in life, we must be aware of others and act responsibly with regard to them and to ourselves.

PART ONE

THE PROBLEM OF POOR
SELF-ESTEEM

Chapter One

Poor Self-Esteem

Of all of the traps and pitfalls in life, self-esteem is the deadliest, and the hardest to overcome; for it is a pit designed and dug by our own hands, summed up in the phrase "It's no use-I can't do it."

—Maxwell Maltz

How Poor Self-Esteem Affects Your Life

Poor self-esteem is the most significant emotional problem that most people have, and a sizeable minority of people feel bad about themselves most of the time. The self-esteem of most people is quite vulnerable to our frequent self-criticism and plummets with experiences of rejection and failure. Having poor self-esteem is very painful, every waking moment of every day. How we feel about ourselves is also an extremely important determinant of the quality of our lives, and it affects our success or failure every day. If we feel good about ourselves, then generally we will expect to succeed, and we will have a better chance of succeeding than someone who expects to fail. Our self-esteem and self-confidence will determine our life goals to a significant degree.

Self-esteem influences how we relate to other people. A person with good self-esteem respects himself and expects others to respect him, too, and he expects others to respond reasonably and generally positively to him. Someone with poor self-esteem sees himself as inferior to others in general and thus expects that others will usually ignore him or respond negatively to him. If you feel bad about yourself, then you will tend to choose someone as a life partner who you think will not reject you, and this will be someone who also has a damaged, negative view of himself or herself.

It was the position of the California Task Force To Promote

Self-Esteem and Personal and Social Responsibility that poor self-esteem is related to engaging in behaviors that are both personally destructive and harmful to society, such as drug and alcohol abuse, unwanted or out-of-wedlock pregnancies, child abuse, family violence, dropping out of school, crime, poverty, and chronic welfare dependence. Since all people seek to feel as good as they can, given their circumstances, and since low self-esteem breeds failure, low self-esteem people are more likely to try other methods than job success and relationship success to feel good, such as using alcohol and drugs to dull emotional pain and feel better temporarily, getting pregnant out of wedlock in order to have a baby who will love one, and sexual promiscuity in an effort to gain at least the good feeling of being wanted by someone for something. People who don't expect to succeed in normal channels and who see themselves as being outside of normal society are more likely to engage in criminal activities. There are other reasons besides self-esteem why people do not have jobs or successful relationships, of course, but how one views oneself and how one values oneself have a great deal to do with whether one has a fulfilling and happy life.

Poor self-esteem begins to form in early childhood. By the age of three, many children are capable of the kind of self-reflection through which they identify or label themselves as "good" or "bad," and this results in good or bad feelings about themselves. Children who feel bad about themselves may appear depressed or may become hyperactive. Most teenagers are troubled by self-esteem problems, as illustrated in their self-doubts and their fears that they may be found to be unacceptable or worthless by their peers. Poor self-esteem is often found in people who do not achieve what society expects or what their families or spouses expect, in terms of getting married, having children, earning a high income, having a high status job, etc. Older adults must deal with the self-esteem insults of the aging process, in which their minds and bodies become less functional and less beautiful (according to our society's definition of what is beautiful and useful).

How Poor Self-Esteem Feels

As an initial common-sense definition, let us say that self-esteem is "how you feel about yourself." A more precise definition will be provided later. Before reading further, take a minute to look within yourself. When you think about yourself, does your reaction have a positive feel to it or a negative feel? Considering every aspect of yourself, is your overall emotional reaction more positive or more negative?

Those with conscious poor self-esteem usually feel ashamed of themselves, dissatisfied with themselves, unhappy with themselves, and as if they were failing in life regardless of their successes. They will tend to see things in a negative light, will expect themselves to mess things up often, and will expect life generally to go badly.

Let's follow a person who feels bad about herself through one day of her life. Anne gets up worrying about what will go wrong that day (and how bad she will feel about herself when it does). Looking at herself in the mirror, she is critical and disappointed with her looks (regardless of how she looks to others). Her husband and children expect her to get them ready to leave for the day, and they treat her in a bossy and critical way. Since she feels bad about herself, Anne tends to see everything that goes wrong as being somehow her fault, and she has communicated this attitude to her family, so that they blame her for every problem.

Anne leaves for work, and at the first stoplight she is acutely aware that she doesn't want others to look at her or her car, since she assumes that if they look they will see something to criticize. She is nervous walking into work since she always half expects people to ignore her or to be annoyed at the sight of her. While working, she tries extra hard, since she has always felt that she was starting from somewhere below everyone else and had to work extra hard to be accepted. It is tiring to worry and try so hard all day. She feels uncomfortable with her fellow workers, seeing herself as inferior and at constant risk of being laughed at or rejected. She does not eat lunch with others, because she sees herself as being not really as good as they are. The only person who associates with her is someone who likes to use her. This person frequently asks Anne to do things for her that should be part of her own work. Anne's need to please in order to make up for her presumed inferiority and her belief that most things are her fault make her a good target for this kind of mistreatment. There are also the little digs by which the "user" reinforces Anne's suspicions that she doesn't look quite right and doesn't have any social standing or rights compared to everyone else. "Oh, it's such a shame that your hair didn't turn out better today," or "You won't be going with us to lunch, so could you take care of this little matter if Mr. Brown calls?" Ann feels unable to defend herself and cannot refuse these requests, since she is desperate to keep her relationships with others positive.

After work Anne worries about whether her family will like what she fixes for dinner. One of her daughters tries to talk to her about feelings of social inadequacy and embarrassment that she is experiencing at school, but Anne knows with a sinking feeling that she can't help her daughter with this, since she herself struggles with the same feelings and worse every day. She is ashamed of her inability to help, since she loves her daughter very much, but all she can do is tell her to keep her spirits up and keep trying. Later that night she is exhausted and tense from the amount of effort it has taken just to get through the day. She doesn't really feel like sex but doesn't have the confidence to say "no" to her husband and so finishes up the day feeling further used, and this confirms her original estimate when she got up that it was going to be a difficult day, that she would feel like a failure no matter what happened, and that she did not really deserve to feel any better than she does already about herself.

It is very painful to live as Anne lives. So much human misery could be alleviated and transformed into enjoyment of life if everyone could feel good about himself or herself! If Anne felt good about herself, she would expect to be respected and generally accepted by her family and her co-workers. She would not take responsibility for others' feelings or duties. She would be comfortable around other people and would feel basically equal to them. She would refuse to be used, put down, or mistreated.

Some might argue that Anne's poor self-esteem is due to depression and anxiety, but I would suggest just the reverse—that Ann is depressed and anxious largely because of how she views herself, what she feels she "deserves" in life, and the daily results for her of these harmful perceptions and beliefs.

Trying to Cope with the Pain of Poor Self-Esteem

When our self-esteem is painful, poor, or damaged we try our best to avoid that pain and to compensate so as to feel better, though these attempts to compensate often create additional problems for us, take extra energy unnecessarily, lead to unnecessary conflicts with others, and become part of "the self-esteem problem."

The most useful (but relatively uncommon) response to feeling bad about oneself is to take actions to improve one's self-esteem level. These actions will be the focus of Parts Two and Four of this book. A far more common response is simply to deny the reality of one's pain and pretend that things are not how they really are. Living in fantasies of a better life and living one's whole life as an act (putting on a false front all the time) would be examples. We can also invent explanations for our pain. For example, if we can fool ourselves into believing that mother said cruel things because she was tired from working all the time, rather than because she didn't love us, it can diminish the pain we feel from the cruel things that she said.

People may try to avoid the pain of poor self-esteem with various distractions, such as being constantly busy, ruminating over other things, "partying," or using alcohol or drugs. Some make up excuses or blame someone else every time they do something wrong or look silly, in order to divert attention from these threats to their self-esteem. Some people try to please others, as if getting positive responses from others would compensate for their poor self-esteem.

By far the most common response to self-esteem pain is to try to feel better about oneself by finding reasons or proofs that one is worthwhile or valuable. We think that if we have these proofs, then we must be worthwhile, and we believe that others will also see us as worthwhile because of these proofs (i.e., "I am financially successful; therefore I must be worthwhile;" or "My mother loves me; therefore I must be OK;" or "If I get elected mayor, then others will think I am important, and it will prove that I'm OK"). People try to use all kinds of proofs—having money, having talents and abilities, having many achievements, having a good job, having possessions, having social status, looking nice, or doing something like skydiving that supposedly illustrates one's courage—anything to look like one is more adequate and valuable than one really feels inside.

Many efforts to prove one's worth depend on claiming that one is "better than" others, such as winning in competition, being like or unlike certain other valued or devalued people, or membership in one's racial group ("I'm white, so I'm better than you"), one's religious group ("I'm Catholic, so I'm better than you"), or one's national group ("Americans are better than other people"). Of course, none of these "proofs" actually prove anything about one's fundamental worth or make one really "better than" anyone else—they are aimed simply at creating a facade of value and OKness. Understanding these efforts to compensate for poor self-esteem will give you a fresh view of status-striving in general and of every effort to be "better than" others.

It is well to note here that some of the behaviors described above can have motives other than compensating for poor self-esteem. A person who wants a Cadillac because he thinks that if he has a Cadillac, others will think he is great, and he can also feel better about himself, is acting to compensate for poor self-esteem. On the other hand, a person who wants a Cadillac because he is convinced that it will be a more comfortable and reliable car for him than other cars is not necessarily trying to raise his self-esteem by getting a Cadillac. The behavior is the same—wanting a Cadillac, but the motive is different.

Homework: What are your "proofs" that you are OK and valuable? Do you believe that you are valuable because your family loves you, or because you have a good job, or because you have a nice car, or because of other reasons? What methods do you use to run from or avoid your painful self-esteem?

Instead of trying to truly improve our self-esteem or fool ourselves and others about our worth, another strategy is to acknowledge the negative characteristics attributed to us or the negative roles that we are cast in (scapegoat, neer-do-well, criminal, geek), but to actively claim to have positive (or at least neutral) self-esteem because of these negative characteristics or roles! An example of this would be a person who says, "Yes, I am not very smart, and I didn't do very well in school, and you [parents, society, etc.] say that that is bad and that I should feel bad about myself because of it, but I don't agree. I'm going to reject your assumptions and feel good about myself instead of bad. Many famous people did poorly in school, and besides those who do well in school are geeks." There is no denial or avoidance of the facts, but there is recognition that the interpretations placed on the facts by others are arbitrary and need not be accepted.

The strategy of recognizing openly who you are but rejecting the negative value judgments made by others about your various aspects and characteristics is a very important one. You are encouraged to use this tactic daily-to accept who you are so completely that you think others' put-downs are silly or stupid.

One final possible response to painful self-esteem is simply to accept one's supposed inferiority and live with it. Images of the hunchback of Notre Dame or the "Elephant Man" or perhaps even Cinderella come to mind. The family scapegoat often accepts that his negative position is what he deserves. Depression and demoralization are expected consequences of accepting chronic bad feelings about the self, and such people typically lead lives of negativity and pain, in social roles that are at the bottom of the status hierarchy, such as vagrant, bum, prostitute, unemployed, or homeless.

Feeling Good About Ourselves is Worth The Effort

Poor self-esteem is a widespread form of human suffering that often leads to chronic patterns of unhappiness and failure and sometimes to serious emotional problems. Our self-esteem determines the quality of our life, and if we suffer every day from feeling bad about ourselves, it would be worth it to recognize this problem and invest in some solutions.

Recognizing the tremendous effort that goes into our attempts to avoid feeling poor self-esteem and to compensate for poor self-esteem will hopefully convince you that it is more beneficial in the long run to actually change your self-esteem than it is to rely on avoidances or compensations to fool yourself and others. In order to do this, we must face up to who we are and to the pain of poor self-esteem, instead of continuing to pretend and lie to ourselves and others.

Pay attention every day to how people try to put themselves above others or get more for themselves by demeaning or degrading others. Pay attention to how they try to deceive themselves and others about who they are and about their value. Recognize and truly understand that every effort to be "better than" someone else may actually be revealing to you the poor self-esteem of the person involved! Apply the same honest examination to yourself, so that you can recognize your own self-deceptions and avoidances. If you see yourself clearly, it will be harder for you to continue to deceive yourself, and you will have more compassion for people as they struggle to deceive others and themselves about who they are so that they can feel better about themselves, if only for a little while.

We are all basically not OK in the sense that we each have our own shortcomings and problems. That is just the way it is. We live in an imperfect world with imperfect people. We do not need to prove that we are OK! It is OK not to be OK. Seeing ourselves as we are and accepting ourselves is the key to feeling better.

Here is a preview of some of the ideas and challenges that this book will pose to you to help you take control of and improve your self-esteem. These ideas may be hard for you to believe, but they are true! This book is dedicated to you being able to believe and actualize every one of these statements and actions in your life.

You deserve good self-esteem.

You can feel good about yourself.

No one is any better than you as a person.

No one has the right to gain advantage over you by putting you down or by claiming to be superior to you.

You are a worthwhile and valuable person regardless of what other people say or feel.

You did not cause bad treatment you may have received from your parents or others in the past, and you are not causing bad treatment others may be giving you now, unless you are directly harming them.

Many people who claim to be or pretend to be superior are actually suffering from poor self-esteem.

You can and should have your own independent ideas and views.

You have no obligation to pretend to be inferior or a scapegoat or to remain in an inferior position just so someone else can feel better.

You have no obligation to remain in a relationship in which the other person damages your self-esteem and will not change that behavior when you request it.

Your relationship with yourself is more important to improving your self-esteem than your relationships with others.

Since you are basically an equal to others, you are worthy of basic respect.

Just because someone else is upset, or is upset with you, it does not automatically mean that you have done something wrong.

If someone else says you are not good enough, he is using the wrong standard.

Doing what is truly best for you is the best way to improve your self-esteem, and it is also the best way to control your behavior.

Homework: Before you read further, you may want to look at the self-esteem evaluation in Part V--Resource 1. I suggest that you fill it out now, so that you will have a relatively unbiased estimate of your self-esteem as it is currently. Later, when you have made some changes in how you look at yourself and how you treat yourself, you can fill it out again to see what changes you have made.

Chapter Two

What Is Self-Esteem?

The most difficult secret for a man to keep is his own opinion of himself.
—Marcel Pagnol

In Chapter One self-esteem was roughly defined as "how you feel about yourself." In this chapter we will develop a more specific and accurate definition of self-esteem. Webster's Ninth New World Dictionary defines self-esteem as "a confidence and satisfaction in oneself" and indicates that it is roughly synonymous with self-respect. Another, less common meaning listed is "self-conceit." Perhaps the most eminent writer in the area, Dr. Nathaniel Branden, describes self-esteem as having two basic components—self-respect and self-confidence. Dr. James Dobson equates self-esteem with a sense of personal worth. Dr. Matthew McKay speaks of self-esteem as being the same as self-worth. Drs. Diane Frey and C. Jesse Carlock define self-esteem as the degree to which one values self, but they also call it a "negative, positive, neutral, [or] ambiguous judgment that one places on the self-concept." The California Task Force To Promote Self-Esteem and Personal and Social Responsibility defined self-esteem as "appreciating my own worth and importance and having the character to be accountable for myself and to act responsibly toward others."

Clearly then self-esteem has something to do with self-respect, self-worth, self-confidence, self-satisfaction, and self-valuing, all of which have emotional components. Frey and Carlock, however, also call self-esteem a judgment, and a judgment is a thought—a cognitive evaluation and conclusion—rather than a feeling. Common everyday language correctly speaks of self-esteem as a feeling, but as we will see again and again, the feeling of self-esteem is determined in part by our thoughts about ourselves. Our thoughts about ourselves form our self-concept, which is the set of thoughts by which we define and understand ourselves (my name is Charles; I look fat; I am an American; I am worthless; etc.).

Self-evaluations are judgments we make about ourselves by comparing our ideas about ourselves with some standard. A boy might say to himself, "Dad said that I did a lousy job cutting the grass, so I must be a pretty poor excuse for a son—I never do things right. I feel like a failure." Clearly then, the standards we use (I should be pleasing to Dad) and the thoughts we have about ourselves affect our self-esteem feelings.

Self-esteem, like self-respect and self-confidence, is a "reflexive" feeling—a feeling that we have "with respect to ourselves." Reflexive feelings or actions involve being both the one who acts and the one who receives the action. In self-esteem, a part of us (the subject) experiences how we feel about ourselves (as the object).

Homework: Let's pause for a moment to take a look inside at your feelings. Look inside yourself and orient yourself toward your feelings about yourself. Let yourself be in touch with the feelings you have about yourself in general, and see what the overall feeling is. This is "how you feel about yourself overall." Good self-esteem is a generally warm, positive, happy feeling about yourself. Poor self-esteem is a painful, negative feeling from which we usually wish to escape.

In order to determine how you feel about yourself, you must first be aware of or observe yourself somehow in order to have a reaction that results in a feeling response. This "look" that we take at ourselves produces some kind of mental content—an image of our physical body or a memory of past successes, etc.—and in response to that content we may feel a feeling based on a previous judgment or previous experience or we may make a new judgment leading to a feeling. Since we have determined that self-esteem is a feeling rather than a thought, then, *self-esteem is a feeling that you have in response to being aware of yourself.*

Sometimes one aspect of yourself looms much larger than any other and will color your response to a question about general self-esteem. If you have just failed an exam, that aspect of yourself would probably be more in the forefront of your awareness, but if you took time, even under the stress of that moment, to get a more general feeling about yourself, you might well come up with a more balanced report. A self-esteem feeling can result from a larger or a smaller aspect of yourself, and your self-esteem also varies over time.

For any given individual, certain areas of function (those that are more highly valued) will be more crucial for overall self-esteem than others. Some people could feel good about most things about themselves but still report overall negative self-esteem because of one really important area in which they felt bad about themselves.

Homework: What areas are more important and less important to your overall self-esteem—physical activity, mental activity, relationships, income, appearance, or other things? Make a list of them and save it for later use when working to improve your self-esteem.

It is extremely important to note that *the external world does not cause the self-esteem feeling directly*. Self-esteem is a feeling we have in response to our perception of ourselves. If my father says he hates me, I may immediately feel some painful emotions (guilt, shame, etc.) from the rejection, but these are not self-esteem pain. I only feel self-esteem pain if I think of myself as a person who is hated by my father and then feel bad about myself for that. "Feeling bad" is not always the same as "feeling bad about yourself."

The terms used to further describe self-esteem (positive, negative, good, poor, neutral) are unfortunately vague and vary in meaning from person to person. Self-esteem is "positive" or "negative" depending on the percentage of self-esteem feelings we have that are either pleasant or unpleasant. It appears that at least as many people have negative overall self-esteem as have positive overall self-esteem. When we have more positive than negative self esteem, we will probably feel "good" about ourselves.

Total vs. Limited-Data Self-Esteem

When one's self-esteem feeling is based on a total look at self (all of one's experiences, abilities, etc.) we will call the result "total self-esteem" (TSE). When one arrives at one's general feeling about self from limited information (a grade on one test, or how one's boyfriend treated one last night), we will call that result "limited-data self-esteem."

In limited-data self-esteem, we make a generalization from a little bit of information about ourselves to a sense of our total selves, and this is often an inappropriate over-generalization. The example was given above of a person feeling generally bad about self after failing a test, when if he thought about his total self, he might very well feel better about himself overall. (Some people may be overwhelmed by the limited-data feelings of the moment and be unable to realize at the same time that there is more to them than the limited data being considered.)

Limited-data self-esteem will obviously be much more variable, depending on immediate circumstances, than total self-esteem, although the accumulation of limited-data feelings in one direction (positive or negative) will eventually lead to a change in total self-esteem in that same direction.

Evaluative (Limited-Test-Data) Self-Esteem

Some of us decide to use only certain key information about the self to determine our self-esteem, thus forming a self-constructed test of whether it is "OK" to feel good about ourselves and whether or not we are "supposed to" feel good about ourselves. In this evaluation of self, one is saying "only if I feel good about these limited areas will I allow myself to feel good about myself overall (regardless of other, more positive data that I could also consider)." An example would be the boy who will only allow himself to feel OK about himself if his mother is happy with him. He might be doing fine in all other respects, but if his mother is unhappy with him, then he will insist on feeling generally bad about himself (until she is happy once again).

We will call this self-imposed test of self-esteem "evaluative" self-esteem (ESE) or "limited-test-data" self-esteem (limited data used as a test for self-esteem). Evaluative self-esteem develops first when a child uses what he knows will please his parents as a self-check for whether he is on track for getting approval, love, and safety, and then manipulates his own self-esteem to prod himself to make things right and guarantee these outcomes.

These tests of self represent aspects of who we believe we are "supposed to be." Examples include "popular," "is loving," "has lots of friends," "gets good grades," "is approved of by mother," "does well at sports," "has lots of money," "is pretty," "has control over others," and so forth. Some people have such difficult tests that their self-esteem is at risk of being low most of the time, particularly if the outcomes are under the control of someone else. An example is the child who is of average intelligence who insists that she will only feel good about herself if she gets all "A's" at school. Since she is probably not capable of getting all "A's" very often, no matter how hard she tries, she is likely to feel bad about herself much of the time.

To maintain our evaluative self-esteem, we have to keep proving ourselves relative to our standards day after day. The fact that one got good grades today and can therefore feel good about oneself does not count for much when the next grades are issued.

Pre-Verbal Self-Esteem

As with other early learning, the self-esteem conditioning of our early years (birth through five) has stronger and more lasting influence on our self-esteem than our later learning. This is probably because early learning is not as subject as later learning to rational evaluation when it is learned, and because the earliest learning (birth to one or two) is pre-verbal and therefore much more difficult to evaluate and change later, because it is difficult to put it into words later so that it can be carefully reconsidered. It will be useful to call the self-esteem that results from this pre-verbal learning "pre-verbal self-esteem."

Biased vs. Objective Self-Esteem

People with poor self-esteem have biased and distorted views of themselves. Other people looking relatively objectively at such people would say that they put themselves down unnecessarily and that when they identify a shortcoming they feel unrealistically negatively about it. Self-esteem that is derived from a relatively negatively biased attitude toward self will be called "negative-bias self-esteem" (or if the tendency is to distort in a positive direction-to pretend that one is better than one really feels—then it is "positive-bias self-esteem"). Non-biased self-esteem is "objective self-esteem".

Socially Destructive and Unhealthy Self-Esteem

No one is inherently any better than anyone else, yet many people cite "reasons" why they are "better than" others in order to bolster their self-esteem, including religious membership, ethnicity, wealth, parentage, and appearance. Being a member of your family may be wonderful, but it does not make you better than anyone else. Similarly, being white or Black or Catholic or Jewish does not make you "better than" anyone else either, but many people cling to the fact that they are of a certain race or religion as "evidence" that they are OK or that they are "better than" someone else.

It is obvious that claiming that one is better than someone else to bolster one's self-esteem will inevitably lead to hurt feelings, resentment, conflict, and struggle. Those who are on the inferior end of the comparison don't like it and will fight back with whatever means are available to them. Inter-group conflicts of all kinds, including wars, involve one group feeling that it is better than the other or that it deserves more than the other (deserves to have some of the other group's land, etc.). The slow but inexorable movement toward equality politically, racially, and between the sexes illustrates the long-term refusal of lower status groups to accept the lower value position assigned to them.

If self-esteem is based on feeling superior or viewing oneself as better than others, for whatever reason, that self-esteem will be called "socially destructive evaluative self-esteem", since it will lead inevitably to social conflict and struggles over superiority. If a characteristic (appearance, race, intelligence, etc.) is used as a justification for self-esteem but not as a reason to feel superior to others, the self-esteem that results will be called "socially non-destructive evaluative self-esteem".

Any self-esteem test or component that leads to more negative than positive self-esteem for the individual, such as using as a test that one get all "A's" in school when one is not mentally equipped to do that, will be viewed in this book as "personally destructive" or "unhealthy" self-esteem. Any self-esteem test that leads one to do self-harming things in order to meet the test involved (harm one's health by staying up all night studying, give up one's friendships in order to please father, etc.) will be viewed in this book as "unhealthy."

What Positive Self-Esteem is Not

True positive self-esteem is not self-conceit, even though it must be acknowledged that feeling good about oneself at the expense of others is used by many as a source of socially destructive self-esteem. There has been insufficient distinction made in the past between socially non-destructive self-esteem, which is neither self-aggrandizing nor aimed at being "better than" others, and those efforts at feeling good about oneself that harm or take away from other people.

Self-esteem is sometimes confused with stubborn selfishness because it is assumed that those who insist on getting their own way must think more highly of themselves and believe that they are more deserving than others. Of course, some people who have good self-esteem may also be selfish, but these are two separate characteristics, since many people with good self-esteem are giving and unselfish. Having good self-esteem means simply that we have positive feelings in response to ourselves, not that we need to get more than others or be superior to others in order to feel good about ourselves.

Some would argue that it would minimize social conflict if we trained everyone to feel bad about themselves, so that they would not assert their needs and wants, and this may be the origin of calling children "bad" in order to get them to conform, as well as the origin of using such notions as original sin to make sure that everyone feels bad about themselves. I would suggest, though, that people who feel unfairly deprived and constrained not to assert themselves openly are more likely to try to get what they want in secret and sneaky ways rather than not to try at all. If we give up our needs in favor of the needs of others, not because we really want to but because we are afraid of being seen as selfish, then we will end up feeling lack of respect for ourselves and hating those who we feel have forced us to give up our needs.

Training people to routinely sacrifice their own needs for those of others is harmful to self-esteem. Unfortunately some religious groups promote this idea. Women, especially, are often expected to sacrifice themselves for the sake of children, husbands, and family. This places them in conflict about also meeting their own needs and is an important contributor to the problems many women have with self-esteem and with chronic depression and minor physical complaints. Any "sacrifice" that is not made freely will result in resentment and other conflicts in the future, and any "sacrifice" that is made freely is not really a sacrifice. Instead of training children in guilt and self-sacrifice, it is better to train them to recognize their needs and those of others and to teach them how to compromise so that everyone can meet his and her needs to a "reasonable" extent at the same time.

Occasionally self-esteem is confused with assertiveness, when it is assumed that anyone who is assertive must feel OK about himself. Being assertive (or aggressive) is one natural reaction to feeling deprived, but the assertive individual can still feel inferior, undeserving, and resentful even when getting what he seeks.

Finally, self-esteem can certainly not be measured by what people claim about their own worth or value. As mentioned above, much status striving is for the purpose of feeling that one is better than others, but this very striving usually betrays poor self-esteem. Some of the contradictory findings in psychological research about self-esteem have resulted from taking at face value the external self-representations of narcissistic and antisocial persons, both of whom frequently claim that they are more valuable than they really feel under the surface. (Remember, self-esteem is not the same as selfishness.)

Homework: To close our discussion of defining self-esteem, I suggest that you take a few minutes to ponder and try to answer the following questions. Try to be as honest as you can, and take this opportunity to be honest with yourself as perhaps you have never been before. One of the essentials for having positive self-esteem is accepting yourself completely. This does not mean that you have to like everything about yourself, but it does mean recognizing and acknowledging everything about you. Being honest with yourself will help you to begin this process of accepting the real you.

Take at least a minute to clear your mind. (It helps to close your eyes and get in a relaxed position physically.) Then focus your attention on a general sense of yourself overall. Try to sense how you feel in response to yourself. Let yourself take some time for various feelings to come up. You may not like some of them, but it is important to make an honest start in finding out how you really feel about you.

Is how you act and treat yourself consistent with how you truly feel about yourself? Do you try to make it look to others as if you respect yourself and feel valuable, when in fact inside you don't feel good about yourself?

Can you distinguish your total self-esteem from your evaluative self-esteem? Do you feel good about yourself in a general way? Do you nearly always feel that you have to be doing or achieving something, or giving a certain impression to others, in order to be OK?

What proportion of your good feelings about yourself is the result simply of you feeling good about yourself (unrelated to other people), and what proportion is due to you feeling good about yourself because someone else feels good about you?

What evaluative standards do you use to determine whether it is OK to feel good about yourself? Make a list of the most important ones. Try to identify where you got those standards.

How much of the time do you succeed in meeting these evaluative standards well enough that you are able to feel good about yourself from an ESE standpoint? What specifically do you often end up feeling bad about?

Do you try to feel better about yourself by feeling "better than" others? How do you try to set yourself up as superior to others? Do you notice ways in which your attempts to feel superior result in conflicts with others?

Do you tend to blame things on others that are at least partly the result of your own choices and actions, in an effort not to feel bad about yourself? How do you usually do this—blowing up in anger, pulling rank, character assassination, scapegoating others, or other ways?

How Can We Recognize Positive Self-Esteem?

Since we cannot actually observe or measure the process inside people of feeling good in response to the awareness of self, and since at this time we do not have adequate research data to verify the various components and behavioral results of self-esteem, for practical purposes we must rely on our good judgment to do this. Identifying the results of positive self-esteem will help us to identify ways to improve our self-esteem. The characteristics below are of people with positive self-esteem.

People with positive self-esteem have positive attitudes, beliefs, and assumptions about themselves, particularly in the following six ways.

1. People with positive self-esteem perceive themselves to be valuable and worthwhile.
2. People with positive self-esteem know that they have a right to exist.
3. People with positive self-esteem believe that they have the right to be their own unique selves, as long as that does not harm or injure others.
4. People with positive self-esteem believe themselves to be and see themselves as being fundamentally the equal of other people

with respect to basic rights.
5. People with positive self-esteem believe that they have just as much right as other people to the good things available in life to all.
6. People with positive self-esteem are satisfied with themselves, even when there are things about themselves that they still wish to improve.

People with positive self-esteem, by definition, have generally positive feeling reactions to themselves, but they are particularly likely to feel these five positive feelings-respecting themselves; accepting themselves as they are; liking themselves; loving themselves; and feeling pleasure and enjoyment from being themselves.

People with positive self-esteem deal with issues of standards and expectations in healthy, self-affirming ways.

People with positive self-esteem do not use harsh self-judgment, self-criticism, and self-punishment as primary means of controlling their own behavior (because these would negatively impact their self-esteem).

People with positive self-esteem do not automatically feel bad about themselves just because of the negative reactions of others or because they have violated the expectations and standards of others, but rather they take control of deciding for themselves whether they have acted inappropriately and whether to feel bad or to change their behavior.

People with positive self-esteem take responsibility for establishing for themselves expectations and standards that are humane, appropriate, and reasonable.

People with positive self-esteem treat themselves well. They make sure to meet their needs at a level acceptable to them. They take good care of themselves, because they deserve good care. They are nice to themselves in various ways, including being kind to themselves, doing good things for themselves, comforting themselves when comfort is needed, and being trustworthy and responsible toward themselves.

People with positive self-esteem have realistically positive expectations and attitudes toward the environment and the future.

People with positive self-esteem expect esteem, respect, and acceptance from others in most circumstances.

People with positive self-esteem have a general confidence in themselves as persons (in contrast to confidence simply in their abilities).

People with positive self-esteem expect and seek appropriate treatment from others. They insist on respect from others. They insist on being treated basically as an equal by others. They do not passively tolerate abuse, ill treatment, or damage to their self-esteem by others. They assert their worth and value in response to societal attitudes and values which act against their self-esteem.

Homework: Consider each of the above descriptions of the behavioral and emotional results of positive self-esteem, and decide whether you have it in your life. Watch other people and recognize these indications of good self-esteem in others.

Chapter Three

How Our Minds Create Self-Esteem

Look well into thyself, there is a source, which will always spring up if thou will always look there.

—Marcus Aurelius

There are six different internal processes by which feelings about ourselves are established.

Basic Association

As infants we associate with ourselves the feelings we have in response to our experiences of being fed, bathed, comforted, etc. If we cry because we are hungry, and mother comes reasonably quickly and satisfies our hunger, we begin to associate mother's face with the pleasure of having our hunger satisfied. Later, we associate our own hunger with mother's face and with the pleasure of being fed, so that whenever we feel hungry, we feel a little bit of the pleasure of being fed, in advance of actually being fed. If these anticipatory sensations are positive, then we are feeling something positive in response to an awareness of ourselves (our hunger), and this is positive self-esteem.

Attributing Experiences to Ourselves

Later, the baby begins to try to consciously understand what causes events to occur, and because babies "believe" that they are the "cause" of everything that happens (that they are "the center of the universe"), they think that their own actions (crying, hunger) cause mother to come and feed them. If these experiences are positive, they will associate themselves (their crying, hunger) with these positive experiences, thus creating some positive self-esteem. The difference between this and the basic association above is that basic association learning is unconscious (occurs without thought or awareness), while causal attributions are conscious.

Attributing Parental Emotions to Ourselves

Around age one, children begin to sense and conceptualize the emotions of others. They tend to attribute to themselves the emotions of their parents—both the emotions that parents display in response to the child (happy, sad, disappointed, etc.) and the general emotional states of the parents (happy, depressed, etc.). If a parent is emotionally distant, then the child will sense that distance and will often attribute it to himself, as if he caused it, and he will feel bad about himself for it. This attribution tendency continues into adulthood for most people— for example, many people believe that if a significant other leaves them, it is because there is something "wrong" with them, instead of assuming that the significant other is responding to his or her own needs and feelings, and that they have not necessarily caused the problem.

Modeling Parental Emotions and Behaviors Toward Us

Children learn a great deal through imitation or modeling, and this includes modeling the emotions and behaviors that parents have toward them. If the parent always frowns when seeing the child, the child will learn to frown and feel tension or distaste in response to herself also. If the parent always smiles on seeing the child, the child will learn to smile and feel pleased and positive in response to herself.

When children are first learning to have some conscious self-control, you will often hear them telling themselves the same words they have heard from parents—saying to themselves for instance, "Johnny mustn't do that," or "Bad Johnny!" or "You're stupid." We tend to punish ourselves in the same ways that our parents punished us.

Modeling the Emotions and Behaviors of Parents Toward Themselves

Children also imitate the emotions that parents have toward themselves and how parents treat themselves. If a child sees mother feeling bad about herself, to some extent she will imitate this way of feeling about the self.

It might seem odd that a child would imitate feelings and behaviors that are painful, but children will do almost anything to be accepted, and if we are similar to our parents, there is a much greater chance that we will be accepted by them. Being like our parents usually produces more good feelings overall than the self-esteem pain we may feel as a result of being like them.

Associating with Ourselves the Good Outcomes We Cause for Ourselves

We associate ourselves with the good feelings that we create for ourselves, and we attribute those good feelings to ourselves as their cause. A child who feels thirsty and as a result gets up and walks to the sink, reaches up to get a glass, turns on the water, fills the glass, and drinks the water, thereby gratifying her thirst, is on the way to associating herself (her own feelings and actions) with the pleasure of satisfying her thirst. (This is the method by which we have the greatest potential as adults to consciously improve our self-esteem, because we have greater control over it.)

Implications for Improving Self-Esteem

As adults, these same six processes still operate to influence our self-esteem, but as adults we are able to evaluate things for ourselves (using our independent minds), and we are better able to escape from people and environments that are harming our self-esteem!

In order to reverse incorrect learning, we can give ourselves enough positive experiences to turn our negative associations into positive ones. In order to change incorrect attributions, we can use our adult minds to understand and interpret these earlier negative experiences in a different way (like correctly telling ourselves that we were not responsible for how our parents treated us).

Self-esteem problems resulting from modeling and making bad outcomes for ourselves are corrected by consciously recognizing our behavior that is hurting us and purposely planning and doing things that are good for us, such as comforting ourselves when we need it instead of punishing ourselves for the sin of "feeling sorry for ourselves."

Homework: Did your parents' reactions make you feel as if your needs and feelings were OK, or did their reactions frighten you and make you feel like hiding your needs and feelings so as to protect yourself?

Do you feel that just by being who you are you cause negative or disapproving reactions in others? What is there about you that is so bad that it causes these reactions? What three things about yourself are you most ashamed of or guilty about? How did your parents criticize you as a child? What did they say or do?

How are your feelings about yourself similar to the feelings your parents had about you? How are the ways you treat yourself now similar to the ways your parents treated you?

How are your feelings about yourself similar to the feelings your parents had about themselves? How are the ways you treat yourself now similar to the ways your parents treated themselves (especially in terms of what they believed they deserved in life)?

Do you feel good about the good things you do for yourself?

Chapter Four

How Our Parents Influence Our Self-Esteem

You cannot teach a child to take care of himself unless you will let him try to take care of himself. He will make mistakes; and out of those mistakes will come his wisdom.

—Henry Ward Beecher

A Major Influence

Our parents have an enormous influence on our later self-esteem, since their behavior shapes our initial ideas about ourselves and our earliest emotional associations to ourselves, at a time in life when we are most easily influenced. Experiences and events outside the family also have considerable influence on self-esteem, but parents have the first and the greatest opportunity to affect our attitudes and feelings about ourselves. Coming to understand the influence of your parents on your self-esteem may enable you to stop blaming yourself for your unhappiness and poor self-esteem.

In growing up, children must learn behaviors that are acceptable to others but that are somewhat arbitrary and particular to each family and each culture and are therefore not the natural way any of us would do them as children (e.g., conventional methods of eating, elimination, times to sleep, etc.), and in this training process the child can hardly help but feel that her natural needs and feelings are being rejected and disapproved. This rejection and disapproval naturally lead the child in the direction of feeling bad in response to self. Because parents must train children behaviorally (using fear, withdrawal, and punishments to some degree) at a time when discussion, self-control, and logic are least effective, almost every one of us has some self-esteem problems! The extent of our problems depends on how well our parents were able to give us positive experiences important for developing good self-esteem, while at the same time helping us handle frustrations and punishments in ways that were least damaging to our later self-esteem.

Most of us have some feelings and attitudes as adults that we had to adopt for the sake of our relationship with our parents but which now are harmful to our self-esteem. An example might be that most children feel that they must submit to authority, whether or not they "understand" what the authority figure is asking of them, but as an adult if you treat every other adult as an authority figure and automatically submit to the will of others, then your self-esteem will suffer significantly. We give no formal help to young adults in changing these childlike attitudes to those more appropriate for adults. I believe that the principles in this book should be taught in school or in other contexts in society to help repair the inevitable damage to self-esteem that occurs naturally as a result of the normal childrearing and socialization processes and to help each of us make the transition from childhood to adulthood more successfully.

In the previous chapter we described general ways in which how parents treat us and how we imitate them affect our self-esteem. In this chapter more specific parental behaviors and attitudes will be identified.

How Parental Feelings and Behaviors Can Harm Self-Esteem

If parents do not want a child, the child will almost always attribute this to herself and will feel inadequate and unworthy (not "good enough" to be loved and accepted).

If parents ignore the child's needs or respond roughly and harshly when they do respond, it gives the child the message that his needs are unimportant or should not be expressed (and therefore that he himself is not important).

When a parent is anxious about parenting, the child will sense this and may associate this anxiety with her needs to be close and feel that there is something wrong with these needs.

Some parents are not able to notice, recognize, attend to, or love their children, due to the parents' self-absorption, narcissism, or emotional problems—once again resulting in the child feeling unimportant, invisible, undeserving, and inferior.

Parents who are not able to accept a child's needs, feelings, and behavior will produce a child who feels "bad," wrong, and undeserving. These parents are always telling their children that they shouldn't want what they want, shouldn't feel what they feel, and shouldn't do what they do.

Parents who consistently put their own needs above those of the child will create children who feel unimportant and inferior. Also, parents who insist that children "honor" them by obeying without question, even if the children are being harmed in the process, are damaging their children's self-esteem.

Some parents withhold from children, both materially and emotionally, because of jealousy or other issues and needs.

Some parents, because they cannot bear for their children to feel better than they themselves do, must actively make the child feel inferior, by shaming, put-downs, or withholding affection or goods from the child. Shaming messages such as "That's stupid," "You'll never be able to do that," and "You'll never be any good at that," will affect self-esteem. Messages of chronic inadequacy are also very available in our schools, where children's personal worth becomes inevitably associated in their minds with their school achievements.

Some parents constantly label their children as "bad," and these children may attempt to disown or hide the parts of themselves that they think are 'bad.'

When a parent blames a child for the parent's unhappiness in life ("I would have been so much better off if you hadn't been born;" "I'll be so glad when you are out of here;" "I hate having you around;" "I wish you were dead"), the child will feel "bad" and very undeserving. A few of these children grow up to be chronically or episodically suicidal, because they believe that they are supposed to be dead, or they may be "accident prone," repeatedly putting their safety and their very lives in jeopardy.

When a parent treats a child violently and abusively, either physically or emotionally, self-esteem can be severely damaged.

When parental expectations and standards are inconsistent or are not specified clearly, the child does not know what will please her parents, and she is likely to feel inadequate and insecure. When parental standards are so high that the child cannot meet them, she will usually just give up and resign herself to a failure role in life.

In some families parental love is so conditional (given only if the child acts in certain required ways) that the child must pretend to be someone other than who he really is most of the time, and the child will end up either with a false identity as a result of pretending to be someone else, or with little or no identity at all, feeling empty, unacceptable, and as if he doesn't know who he is. Clearly, a child who believes that he is valued regardless of performance, just for himself, will be much more secure than a child whose support in the world can change from moment to moment, based on someone else's evaluations and feelings.

Some parents will accept the child only if the child gives up his own separate identity and stays "fused" with the parent, as if they were one person rather than two. Some parents will accept a child only if the child agrees with the parents' distortions of reality. Children who give up their identities, separateness, and good judgment cannot have good self-esteem, because they do not have a separate self with which to associate good outcomes.

If parents feel bad about themselves, then the child may model this pattern and feel bad about himself. If parents exhibit mostly negative feelings toward the child, the child will grow up modeling these feelings and feeling mostly negative toward himself.

Sometimes parental behaviors per se do not initiate the parent-child problem. There are children whose inborn temperament differs from their parents and make them hard to live with and hard to love. Some children reject loving and physical contact or seem impossible to comfort. Sometimes parents cannot overcome these differences, even when they try their best. In these cases empathy and understanding are usually difficult for both parent and child, which makes communication and acceptance difficult as well. The child will often feel alien and unaffirmed, if not outright rejected and unloved. The impact on self-esteem is obvious.

How To Help a Child Develop Positive Self-Esteem

Meet your child's needs reasonably, promptly, and reliably, so that the child accepts and becomes comfortable with his needs. Don't make your needs (or those of anyone else) systematically more important than the child's needs, for if you do, you will teach the child that he is inferior.

Accept your child's feelings as a natural part of him. Don't make them "bad" in an effort to control his behavior. Help him to control the expression of his feelings by teaching him adaptive ways to manage feelings and by showing him how you do this. Accept that it takes children years to learn to manage their feelings.

Be trustworthy and responsible toward your child, thus demonstrating that she is worth treating well.

Make it clear that the child has a definite and irrevocable right to exist in this world, by taking the child's needs seriously and communicating that he is important to you.

By recognizing, acknowledging, accepting, and praising the child's personality and unique traits and abilities, give the child the message that he has the right to be exactly who he is, and that to be himself is a great thing.

Convey to the child, verbally and non-verbally, that she is valuable, worthwhile, important, and deserving of nurturance and good things in life.

Respect your child's equal rights and basic equality with others (including you) at all times and in all circumstances, without exception.

Act toward your child with respect at all times, just as you would show respect to an adult and would want respect from others yourself.

Give affection and love generously, including safe, appropriate, and loving physical contact.

Accept your child as he is, with his own needs, feelings, and behaviors. Help him find a way both to be himself and to be socially acceptable. Don't pressure him to be someone he is not. Accept the ways in which the child is different from you, and don't force him to be just like you.

Be satisfied with your child.

Help your child construct a positive self-concept by verbalizing positive perceptions of the child whenever possible.

Help your child construct an accurate self-concept by helping him recognize his negative and his positive behaviors and traits.

Do not use the overly simple and terribly destructive labels of "good" and "bad" on your child. You can communicate your love or your displeasure clearly without these words, and you can reinforce behavior adequately without them.

Hold clear, consistent, and appropriate expectations and standards for your child that he can readily understand and, with appropriate effort, can readily meet.

Praise and encourage your child's efforts and successes.

Provide comfort and support in times of frustration and failure, so that she can learn to comfort herself.

Help your child to learn that while certain behavioral standards must be obeyed, all human standards are the opinions of fallible men and women and should be questioned or replaced when more humane and reasonable standards are possible and appropriate.

In showing disapproval as a method of training a child, help the child to understand that it is his behavior that is unacceptable, rather than himself as a person.

Help your child to judge accurately the difference between when another person's feelings are hurt and when that person is actually harmed, and to assess realistically whether he himself has harmed the other person (instead of assuming that any time someone else is upset or "hurt" that he must have done something wrong).

Help your child not to automatically "feel bad" just because another person is upset with her or wants her to be different.

As your child grows, encourage your child to think hard enough about right, wrong, good, and bad, to construct—using the basic values that you have taught—his own standards and values.

Show your child how to meet her own needs by taking good care of yourself, meeting your needs acceptably, and doing good things for yourself.

Show your child how to be nice to himself, by loving yourself, being kind to yourself, and comforting yourself.

Give special support to children who have been victims of trauma or who for some reason receive chronically negative messages about themselves.

Help your child learn the skills needed in order to get along well with others and to get what she needs from others, in positive, mutually beneficial relationships.

Help your child to insist on basic equality with others in the world and not to settle for less.

Help your child develop appropriate assertiveness skills, to support the various requests and demands he must make of the world.

Help your child see the wisdom of leaving punishing, harmful relationships that cannot be improved, in order to seek better relationships in the world.

Help your child to understand what it is to be oneself with integrity—to be true to oneself, to make one's private and public selves as congruent as possible, to stand up for one's values, and to express one's love and enthusiasm for oneself by being oneself completely and with vigor.

Homework: It will be useful now to go back and re-read the previous section while thinking of you as a parent helping *yourself* in these various ways to develop good self-esteem!

The more secure and positive your own self-esteem is, the more you will naturally treat others, including your children, in ways that promote good self-esteem. If you as a parent realize that you are raising your children in ways that are damaging to their self-esteem, you are urged to change those behaviors yourself or seek professional help so that you can make those changes.

Chapter Five

How Society Shapes Our Self-Esteem

If you don't run your own life, somebody else will.
                                                    —John Atkinson

The Influence Of Our Social Environment

Parental caretaking has the earliest and perhaps greatest influence on our self-esteem, but the experiences we have of events beyond our families also shape our self-esteem throughout our lives, including both the life cycle experiences that are common to us all and the influences of living in our own particular society with its particular beliefs and attitudes.

Since we are imperfect human beings with imperfect understanding, and since we are constantly prone to error as well as being at risk constantly for rejection or ill use by others, our self-esteem will always be influenced from outside and can never be impervious to others' input. Moreover, it is important that we pay attention to others' input in case it contains useful information for us, but at the same time rejecting input that is self-serving. We must learn from what happens to us but also develop the strength and skills not to allow negative experiences to lower our self-esteem unnecessarily.

A reasonable goal for us would be to make our self-esteem not impervious to influence but positive and strong enough to carry us through most of the difficult times that will occur to all of us—when we make mistakes, when others are unhappy with us or blame us, and when misfortunes occur.

Life Cycle Events and Issues

Playing with children from other families presents the first challenge to our self-esteem from outside our own families. If we attribute to ourselves (as our "fault") the dislike or mistreatment we get from these other children, then of course our self-esteem will suffer. These play relationships are also our first opportunity to recognize that our family's attitudes, beliefs, and practices are not sacred and are not automatically "better" than those of other families or other groups. They are simply more familiar to us. In dealing with differences, the trick is not to tie your self-esteem too closely to your family's way of doing things (or your society's ways of doing things) but rather to accept that everyone has some rights to choose his or her values and to understand the world according to his or her unique experience, and that the resulting differences need not be felt as a threat most of the time.

Some unfortunate children may be used as scapegoats in families and other groups—the one kid in the group of kids who is always chosen last, who is always the butt of the cruel jokes of the parent or group leader, or who is seen by the rest of the family or group as the weakest, least intelligent, or least capable. The others can feel better about themselves because they view the scapegoat as being "worse" than themselves. (Scapegoats can also serve other purposes, such as being invested with all of the "bad" or "evil" of the group, but we are only interested here in the self-esteem implications.)

School grades and teachers' reactions to us have a tremendous influence on self-esteem, because children may inappropriately interpret grades to be an indication of their overall worth in the eyes of adults, rather than seeing them as only an indication of academic success. Children who get better grades are not "better than" other children, and we must help children see that their worth as persons is not related to their grades! Any child who is making reasonable progress toward being able to support himself in the world and to participate appropriately in society is a success, regardless of grades.

Teenage years are a time of great insecurity, as teenagers try to discover whether they can survive outside their families. Even small rejections by peers seem terrible and have significant influence on their self-esteem.

Adults tend to judge their relative worth by the status of their jobs and by how much money they earn, when clearly income says little about a person's fundamental worth, since income depends just as much on luck and the way jobs are defined in our society as it does on ability. Because women are expected to be homemakers as well as workers, evaluating worth by income is especially unfair to them.

People are often judged by whether they are married and have children. If we cannot find someone to love us, we easily think that there is something wrong with us and feel ashamed or depressed. Parents sometimes unrealistically judge their worth by the success or failure of their children.

Chronologically following marriage and childrearing is the time of "mid-life crisis," when we are confronted with the realization that some of our hopes and goals for our lives are not going to be achieved, and after that comes old age, when because our society is so youth-oriented and death-phobic, many older people feel ignored, degraded, and lonely, in addition to having to deal every day with the realities of old age—that some of their powers are declining and their bodies are slowly failing. Death, of course, puts an end to all of our pretensions to power and effectiveness, but our lives are triumphs in themselves that far outshine the fact that they must come to an end!

In addition to the stresses on self-esteem from these "normal" life issues that we all encounter along the road of life, there are some unusual circumstances that can have a very negative impact on self-esteem, such as losing a parent when one is quite young through death or divorce. Children frequently attribute these losses to themselves or to something they have done and therefore feel bad about themselves. Being abused has a staggering impact on self-esteem. To have the very people who are supposed to love you and take care of you hurt you severely and repeatedly is one of the most traumatic things that can happen to any of us, as well as the most difficult to adjust to or overcome in later life. Severe illness, disfigurement, or amputation can have a severe impact on self-esteem. Often people think—even if only in the back of their minds—that accidents and disease are punishments for wrongdoing, and they attribute the blame to themselves. ("What did I do to deserve this?")

It is worth noting that the solution to these life-cycle self-esteem difficulties is to learn to feel good about ourselves and not worry excessively about pleasing others!

Societal Factors that Affect Self-Esteem

In addition to the impact on self-esteem of how our parents treat us and the normal developmental tasks that we all face in life, your self-esteem is being affected every day, sometimes without your awareness, by aspects of society around you that you may accept as natural and unavoidable. It will benefit you to be aware of these factors, so that you can protect your self-esteem.

Every superiority/inferiority relationship will harm the self-esteem of the person in the inferior position. People who find themselves in the superior position are tempted to base their self-esteem on that superiority, which is a less reliable self-esteem support over the long run than belief in their own fundamental, natural, inherent positive value as a person. Any time a person is put down and seen as inadequate or "not enough," by comparison with someone else or by comparison with a standard, self-esteem will suffer.

Any societal factor that decreases our opportunities for autonomously creating good outcomes for ourselves decreases our opportunities for building good self-esteem. Any societal beliefs or customs that blame the individual in order to control his or her behavior will decrease self-esteem. Examples of this would be having our attempts to love ourselves be called selfish, and children justifying abuse from their parents by misapplying the principle "honor thy father and thy mother." Any societal tendency to identify a person's value only with external, superficial factors (such as age, race, beauty, achievements, wealth, etc.) or with one's value to others, as opposed to one's fundamental positive value as a human being, will degrade total self-esteem.

It should not be assumed from the above that it would be better if people did not have consequences for their behavior. Children must learn to conform to society's already established ways of doing things.

People should work if they are to eat. Standards and laws are necessary. However, it is desirable that damaging the self-esteem of people not be used as a means of teaching or enforcing the rules and standards that we must have.

Self-esteem is supported in general by societal ideals of equality, equal respect for each person, the dignity of each person, and equal opportunity for each person. Ideals of self-determination and self-sufficiency support self-esteem, since they encourage us to take responsibility for ourselves and to do all that we can to make good outcomes for ourselves.

Since human beings naturally create status hierarchies as a part of their social structures, every society develops and institutionalizes many inequalities. The inequalities between men and women are a notable example. If men are more valued or given more privileges, then the self-esteem of women will suffer. Adults are more important than children in our culture, and children have fewer legal rights or protections, so children are at a decided disadvantage with respect to self-esteem. Status based on racial prejudice, religious membership, or other group identifications always degrades the self-esteem of the supposedly "inferior" groups.

Every time status differentials are created, the self-esteem of some will suffer, since those who are seen as superior will receive more goods and admiration than those who are seen as inferior. In truth, football heroes, multimillionaires, and Einstein's do not "deserve" more respect or rewards than anyone else for being athletic, rich, or brilliant (although these individuals may receive more respect and rewards as individuals if they produce unusual benefits for others). Men do not deserve more pay than women just because they are men. Whites do not deserve more pay than Blacks just because they are white. Adults do not deserve more rewards than children just because they are older. The strong do not "deserve" more than the weak, simply for being more powerful. The bad effects on the self-esteem of those in "inferior" positions should be good reason for all of us to stop basing our own self-esteem on being superior to anyone else!

Whenever there are status differentials and whenever some are valued more than others, the self-esteem of those less valued and those lower in status will suffer.

Our society greatly over-emphasizes winning and competition, and we tend to think that winners "deserve more" respect and goods than losers. Winners may get more (or take more), but they do not "deserve" more in general than anyone else. It would be better for all of us if we were to focus on admiring effort and skill and make winning less important.

Advertising in our consumer society strives to influence our self-esteem and our value by telling us that our value will be enhanced by buying and using advertised products, and that our value will be diminished (we will be undesirable, look stupid, or be uncool) if we do not buy and use those products.

In the increasing amount of time we spend in pure "entertainment" (television, movies, video games, etc.) we focus more and more only on those who in fantasy we would like to be, and by doing this we ignore and therefore demean everyone else, ourselves included. As children we need heroes and people to look up to and emulate, but as adults we should live real lives ourselves and be ready to act as models for our children, rather than fantasizing about being someone else. Everyone can be appropriately seen as a hero in his or her own life!

The more society encourages unthinking conformity to the wishes of authority (so that people will agree, for instance, with complicated and unexplained political policies, or buy ineffective but well-advertised products), the less chance there will be for people to develop self-confidence, self-knowledge, and self-trust and the secure self-esteem that comes from these attributes.

If we treat other people with respect and concern, we will establish conditions that allow the self-esteem of everyone to prosper, but if we are primarily concerned with getting what we can from others, by manipulation or unfair tactics if necessary, then everyone's self-esteem will suffer. The increasing emphasis over the last fifty years on "the bottom line" (degree of profit) as the justification for every business decision has resulted in loss of respect for employers, to whom the welfare of their employees as persons (not just as means to the company's ends) has become less and less important.

Self-esteem and the value of each individual person are degraded in our society to the extent that we tolerate the attitudes that it is OK to get what you want from others by putting them down, lying to them, violating their rights, or otherwise manipulating them.

The increasing interdependence, specialization, and complexity in our society make self-esteem more difficult, because the less we can do autonomously for ourselves, the more difficult it is to associate ourselves and our actions with the positive outcomes we obtain. In addition, we are creating a larger and larger class of people in our society who can no longer produce at the levels demanded for employment and are simply cast aside—jobless and often homeless. Unfortunately, our belief that everyone can succeed if they would only try leads to blaming and disrespecting those who do not succeed, even in those cases in which it is not reasonable to see it as their "fault."

Parents are becoming less certain about how to raise children and what to teach them, because they are less certain about their values and what choices in life will best move them toward their goals, and children are having more difficulty achieving adult self-respect because it is so much more difficult to make the economic transition from their families to taking care of themselves now than it was in the past (because they are used to a lifestyle in their families that as beginning wage-earners they cannot support by themselves).

Our strong motivation to avoid all pain inevitably decreases our self-confidence in our ability to meet the demands of real life, since real life clearly involves pain.

Our "entertainment society" tends to turn us into spectators instead of participants in life, so that we lose opportunities for self-expression, for gratifying each other, and for creating good outcomes for ourselves because we watch others do things instead of doing those activities ourselves, often out of fear that we will not be "good enough."

Our materialism and over-emphasis on possessions give the impression that things are more important than people, thus diminishing the value of each person.

The faith that ever increasing amounts of education would increase everyone's income has led to lengthening everyone's childhood by requiring every child to stay in academically-oriented school the same length of time. This results in a great deal of wasted time and lower self-esteem for those youths who are not learning academically and do not want this kind of education. It would be better for their self-esteem to be able to work earlier in life as apprentices or to go to true trade schools earlier, in order to make good use of their adolescence in preparing for earning a living.

Cultural Differences

The analysis in this chapter is of Western European/United States society and the factors in this society that support or degrade self-esteem. The values and views of what is socially appropriate are, of course, different in other cultures. For example, one might perceive the comments in this chapter as supporting an individualistic view of emotional health rather than a group-oriented view (in which the individual's place in and contribution to the group are more important than her self-development and personal achievements). The self-esteem principle is the same, though, in all cultures, since people are the same the world over. To the extent that one views oneself positively and makes good outcomes for oneself, self-esteem is increased. In both individualistic and group-oriented systems, we must act in ways that we believe are in our best interest or our mental health will suffer.

In group-oriented systems, the individual believes that the maintenance of group harmony and balance are of primary importance and are directly in her best interest, so acting to support that, even when it ignores what in another culture might be her personal preferences, creates positive associations between the individual and her choices and actions (and therefore positive self-esteem). In both individualistic and group-oriented systems, to the extent that individuals act in accordance with societal expectations but believe that this is not in their individual best interest, their self-esteem will decline.

To belong to and contribute to the maintenance of any group involves some denial of self for the sake of the welfare of the group. As long as the individual believes wholeheartedly that this denial of self is in his own best interest, then it does not take away from his sense of purpose and his happiness with himself for contributing to his own welfare. However, if this denial of self leads to depression, dysfunction, or somatic problems, then it is excessive (at least for that individual), and some change is needed.

Neither the group nor the individual is supreme. Sacrificing the individual for the sake of the group is not morally superior to sacrificing the group for the sake of the individual. Both world views, in their pure or extreme forms, pose problems for maximum self-esteem. Total adherence to individual gain is actually counterproductive for the individual, since it does not take into account the resulting losses in relational benefits and the resulting goal-attainment failures due to failures to cooperate. Total adherence to group benefit regardless of individual welfare, on the other hand, leads to hypocrisy and anger (conscious or unconscious), since the human organism is constructed with the imperative to maintain itself first. Perfect submission to the group also involves giving up the personal struggle to define what is good and right (since the individual accepts the group's definition of what is good and right), and if all the individuals in the group defer to the group to define what is good and right, then the "group mind" (sometimes the mob) determines what is good. Perfect submission to the group, then, does not necessarily have morally desirable outcomes. Finding a workable balance for the human organism between individual benefit and group welfare is the goal of culture.

Self-Esteem Through Individual Efforts Versus Self-Esteem Through Interactions with Others

Some readers may be concerned that this book seems to be separating self-esteem from our relationships with others, and there is some truth to this. In my opinion, our good feelings come from gratifications of our needs, our feelings in response to ourselves, and our feelings in interactions with others. All good feelings do not come from relationships. Also, some relationships are destructive to self-esteem. (If everyone treated everyone else with respect and acceptance, there would be no self-esteem problems!) This book presents methods for those who are not getting sufficient respect and acceptance from others to be able to increase their overall good feelings by improving the quality of their responses to themselves.

Changing Society

As you have probably realized, the fundamental issues underlying the various life-cycle and societal factors described are (1) striving for superiority over others, (2) treating each other in demeaning, degrading ways, and (3) choosing courses of action that are not good for our self-esteem but have other pay-offs that we want (holding onto a relationship, higher income, more immediate pleasure, etc.). We do these things in order to get more for ourselves and to get more than others have, and therefore to feel better about ourselves. These habits are rooted in family experiences in which we felt we had to compete in order to survive or to get what we wanted, and in which mistreatment of others as a means of striving was tolerated or even encouraged. Many people stop their moral and ethical learning at this childish level of "devil take the hindmost" and continue to treat everyone in this self-centered way.

We need to understand now that while this sort of striving to get ahead by pushing others down was the only way we knew how to cope as children, its results in adults are more destructive than they are helpful. Accepting and loving ourselves for just being ourselves, and having good self-esteem as a result, can start us on a path toward insisting on a "growing up" of our society, that will include everyone insisting on good treatment from others and everyone consistently treating others well, too, because this mode of interaction will actually bring all of us better self-esteem, more satisfaction, greater fulfillment and less pain than the old ways.

Chapter Six

Everything You Need To Know About Improving Self-Esteem

The greatest discovery of my generation is that man can alter his life simply by altering his attitude of mind.

—William James

You Can Improve Your Self-Esteem

This chapter presents a comprehensive program for improving and maintaining your self-esteem, involving compassion for yourself (and others) and learning to make your own decisions about what is right and true. There is a lot to learn, but don't feel overwhelmed. Any journey begins with a first step, and every skill you develop for yourself will make acquiring others that much easier.

To work on improving self-esteem, we will focus frequently on evaluative (limited-data) self-esteem, even though the ultimate goal is to increase your total self-esteem and thereby minimize the need for finding reasons to feel good about yourself. Focusing on improving our evaluative self-esteem has great potential for increasing our awareness of our self-esteem problems and for showing us what we must do to improve. For example, if you try to be nice to yourself but you don't feel that you deserve nice treatment, you will be faced with this attitude toward yourself when you try to treat yourself nicely. Each time you become aware of a negative attitude toward yourself or of how you judge yourself, you have the opportunity to become more accepting and compassionate toward yourself, and this will make your total self-esteem just a little bit stronger. Gradually we can become less and less dependent on evaluating ourselves according to how others treated us or according to inappropriate standards from the past.

The twelve steps for developing positive self-esteem.

1. **Declare Independence For Your Mind** — In order to make good choices and get what you want in life, you must see reality as it actually is, rather than how others say it is. In order to see the truth and be realistic, you must develop your independent mind. You must be willing to see the truth about yourself and about others, even when it is unpleasant, because having your own independent and accurate view of reality is the key to being able to know your own enduring value.

2. **You Have Fundamental Value Independent of Others**— When you are able to have your own independent view of things, you can separate yourself from what others say or feel about you. Instead of viewing yourself as valuable or worthless according to what other people say or feel, you can understand others' idiosyncratic views as their own, and you can hang onto your own sense of value and worth, even when you are criticized or rejected.

3. **You Are Basically Equal To and Not Inferior To Others**— When you can understand that you never were inferior or worthless, no matter what others said or how they treated you, then you can claim your own equality with others. You are basically equal to others in terms of deserving the same basic respect, rights, opportunities, and share of the pie as everyone else.

4. **You Did Not Deserve To Be Treated Badly**—If you have felt that you deserved the bad treatment you received, you must re-think this. It is time to realize that no child deserves mistreatment and that if you were mistreated or treated as inferior, it was due to the problems of others and not to any inferiority or lack of value in yourself. Understanding this, you can stop blaming yourself for your poor self-esteem.

5. **You Have the Right To Exist and To Be Yourself**—Since you are basically an equal, you have just as much right as everyone else to be in this world and just as much right to be yourself (as long as you are not directly harming others).

6. **Respect Yourself**—As an equal, you deserve basic respect. You should treat yourself with respect at all times just as you would any other person who deserved respect, and you should insist on being treated with respect by others.

7. **Accept Yourself (and Forgive Yourself)**—Stop rejecting yourself. Let yourself be. All parts of yourself deserve your acceptance (even if you want to change some of them). Forgive yourself for ways in which you have accepted an inferior position up to now.

8. **Love Yourself**—You deserve respect, acceptance, and love-especially your own love. Learn to treasure and love yourself, and treat yourself lovingly and compassionately at all times.

9. **You're Not Perfect But You're Perfectly Good Enough**— If others say you are not good enough, they are using the wrong standards! If you or others have held unrealistic expectations for you, it is time to reject those unrealistic expectations and standards, adopt reasonable standards, and accept yourself as being OK and good enough. As long as you are doing your best to take care of yourself and are treating others decently, you are good enough.

10. **Do What Is Truly Best for You**—Decide on your behaviors and choices on the basis of doing what is truly best for yourself. (This will require taking into account all of the future consequences of your actions, including how others will be affected by those actions.)

11. **Treat Yourself Well**—If you are to love yourself and think well of yourself, you must treat yourself well. You are a treasure, and you deserve good treatment.

12. **Ensure that Others Treat You Well**—In order to think well of yourself and love yourself, you will need to do your best to encourage others to treat you well. You (just like every other person) deserve decent, fair, equal treatment, and you must assert this right when others treat you badly or as being inferior.

The Comprehensive Self-Esteem Program

The remainder of this book will explain the above 12 steps. In order to see these steps in context, here is a description of all aspects of the program.

Know yourself. (If you do not know yourself completely and accurately, you will not be able to make good choices or to understand and therefore correct your behavior.)

Be accurately, realistically, and completely aware of everything within you—your needs, wants, feelings, thoughts, perceptions, motives, and potentials. Be honest with yourself and know everything about yourself, regardless of whether it is valued by you or others. Be aware of the things about yourself that you dislike, without judging them. Resolve never to lie to yourself, pretend to yourself, or deceive yourself about yourself.

Understand yourself, your motives, and know how and why you react to things as you do. This knowledge will help you to see how you avoid knowing the truth about yourself and about other people, their motives, and their behavior toward you. It will also keep you aware of when you turn away from the more difficult aspects of personal change, so that you can get yourself back on the path to better self-esteem when you need to.

Understand the difference between your value as a person and the responses of others to you. Learn to understand others' communications as their personal viewpoints, and refuse to accept feedback about you as true just because someone else says it. Your value is not at all the same as how others respond to you—you have immense value to yourself and significant value to certain other people, even if most of the three billion people in the world care nothing about you or devalue you for their own reasons. Never take what others say, think, or feel about you or in response to you at face value. Recognize and filter out the manipulations and unreasonableness in others' communications about you and their responses to you, so your self-esteem does not suffer.

Understand your impact on others accurately, neither minimizing it nor exaggerating it. We need to understand how we affect others in order to distinguish the reasonable responses that others have to us from their unreasonable or idiosyncratic reactions.

Make an appropriate break with the unhappy and unhealthy past and develop attitudes and motivation that will support your growth.

Give up your dependence on others for your self-esteem. Make the shift from looking to others' reactions for how to feel about yourself, to looking to your own feelings and humane perceptions of yourself as the main sources of your self-esteem.

Give up your previous unhealthy methods of attempting to compensate for poor self-esteem. Whether you tried to fool yourself or others about yourself or tried to impress others with position, possessions, power, or personal attributes, detach yourself from these crutches, and learn to feel good about yourself because of your unchanging fundamental worth and for your own reasons—not because of how others react to you. If you have poor self-esteem, then accept that as your current reality. Acknowledging it is the first step toward changing it.

Discard superficial values with regard to self-worth (such as valuing position, possessions, power, appearance) and adopt more meaningful values. Begin to look at everyone in terms of things that matter—how one treats others, whether one is honest and responsible, whether one contributes to others' lives practically or emotionally, how one treats oneself, etc.

Be willing to change and willing to perceive yourself as worthwhile and valuable. We are all afraid of change and its unknowns, but only by moving ahead into unknown territory can we make progress. Be aware when you avoid dealing with your self-esteem issues, and redirect yourself toward change. You may have been trained from childhood to see and think of yourself as worthless and unimportant, but you must now question, challenge, and reject this view of yourself. You are actually the most worthwhile and valuable person in the world to yourself, and every person can be worthwhile and valuable to at least some other people.

Take responsibility for yourself and your self-esteem, and make yourself the chief architect of your self-image, self-concept, and self-esteem. Make a commitment to yourself to improve your self-esteem. Instead of looking to others and how they treat you for how to feel about yourself, begin deciding yourself how you feel about yourself and deciding for yourself how you are going to be affected by how others view you and treat you. Instead of feeling like a victim, with others controlling your feelings about yourself, make yourself responsible for actions that can help you feel better about yourself now. Take control of your feelings about yourself and protect them from the attacks and manipulations of others. Make relating to yourself well and managing your life better your number one priority for the rest of your life.

Be honest with yourself about others (including, as needed, recognition of how others have harmed your self-esteem). No matter how painful it is to see how others have hurt you, especially those you love, don't shrink from this knowledge, but use it to consider how you can improve your life.

Give up believing that something about you causes others to treat you badly and to see you as inferior. (Stop blaming yourself for your poor self-esteem!) See yourself and your behavior more realistically—there is nothing about you that "makes" others treat you badly or view you as inferior.

Cultivate healthy attitudes, beliefs, and assumptions about yourself.

Believe that you have the right to exist. You have the right to exist regardless of how your parents felt about you and regardless of how they treated you. Everyone has this right-it does not have to be earned.

Believe that you have the right to be yourself. You have the right to be yourself, regardless of what others think or feel about that, as long as you are not harming others inappropriately by being yourself. The real you is OK. You don't need to please everyone, and you don't have to please anyone in particular. You will be happiest if you develop your own natural combination of abilities and talents, rather than trying to be what someone else wants you to be. Strive to become yourself, because that is the self that you can love best!

Believe that you are fundamentally the equal of others. You deserve the same basic rights and appropriate treatment that everyone else gets. You are not inferior to others, and no one has the right to define you as inferior. Question yourself every time you take an inferior position yourself or accept the assignment of inferior status by someone else.

Make your needs as important as those of others. Since you are fundamentally equal to others, your needs are just as important as theirs. No one's needs automatically come before yours, unless you allow it. You cannot put the needs of anyone else before yours all the time without resenting that other person, becoming depressed, and hating yourself. Question yourself every time you accept a less than equal share.

Believe that you have the same right as anyone else to the good things available in life to all, including respect and equal and appropriate treatment by others. Since you are fundamentally equal to others, you deserve good things just as much as they do (though not more than they do). Question yourself every time you feel or think that you do not deserve something good.

Be satisfied with yourself. Just as you don't have to be perfect to accept yourself, you don't have to be perfect or be just the way you want to be in order to be satisfied with yourself (which means basically that you are living up to your own expectations). Make sure that your expectations of yourself are reasonable. You are OK right now. (If you are dissatisfied with yourself, you are using the wrong standards!)

Cultivate positive feelings toward yourself.

Respect yourself. Everyone, from the lowest to the highest, deserves basic respect and is equally deserving of basic respect, regardless of status or position. Be respectful of yourself at all times.

Treat yourself and others with respect, and insist that others treat you with respect.

Accept yourself completely, including your thoughts, feelings, needs, motives, behavior, body, potentials, and personality. Self-acceptance (which is basically letting yourself be and not feeling that you must change in order to be OK) is the single thing that will contribute the most to improving your self-esteem. Lack of self-acceptance, and the resulting self-criticism and self-blame, are the biggest enemies of self-esteem. Don't reject any part of yourself. You don't have to be perfect to be acceptable. You may not be happy with some aspects of yourself, and you may want to change some things about yourself, but you can still accept yourself right now just as you are. No matter how others have seen you, and no matter what you have done, you can still accept yourself right now just as you are. Even with all of your faults and warts, you are an acceptable, worthwhile, valuable person.

Like yourself. You are likable.

Love yourself. Respecting, accepting, and loving yourself are the three most beneficial things you can do to improve your relationship with yourself and your self-esteem. You are lovable, just as you are, regardless of what you have done or how you have been treated or defined by others, including your parents. Open your heart and try to love yourself and don't give up until you do. Make your own love even more important than love from others. Become your own best friend, advocate, and supporter.

Take pleasure in being yourself. Learn to enjoy your own company. Pay attention to yourself, and you can find pleasure and enjoyment in just being yourself, in your moment to moment consciousness, in the everyday activities you do, and in the valuable things that you do for yourself.

Deal with standards and expectations in healthy ways, including both the standards and expectations that others have for you and those that you have for yourself. Stop harming your self-esteem through applying inappropriate, unreasonable, or inhumane standards and expectations to yourself.

Stop judging yourself harshly and punitively. While it is necessary to control our behavior in ways that will both get us what we want in society and avoid consequences that we do not want, it is not necessary to judge ourselves harshly and punitively and constantly criticize ourselves in order to control ourselves or to motivate ourselves to "be good" and do the right thing. (An approach based on doing what is best for ourselves is much more humane as well as being perfectly adequate to accomplish the task of controlling our behavior as adults. Doing what is really best for ourselves takes into account all of the long-term and short-term consequences of our behavior as well as our impact on others.)

Stop blaming yourself inappropriately. Persons with poor self-esteem usually blame themselves for whatever goes wrong, and they take nearly total responsibility themselves for their bad lot in life, including their poor self-esteem. It seems natural to blame themselves because it is "natural" for children to believe that either they have done something to deserve the bad treatment they receive or that something about them makes it appropriate for others to treat them badly. This self-blame is almost always inappropriate.

Stop feeling bad about yourself automatically because of the standards, expectations, judgments, feelings, and reactions of others. People with poor self-esteem feel bad and often blame themselves whenever someone else is upset, without evaluating whether they have in fact done anything "wrong." Whenever others are unhappy, and whenever others are unhappy with you or critical of you, you must begin to think and decide, based on your own best judgment, whether you have done something to be sorry for, or whether the other person should be taking responsibility himself for his feelings.

Question all standards. Take control of deciding which standards and expectations are appropriate for you and which you will honor. Question your own standards, your family's standards, and society's standards, and evaluate them for yourself according to how reasonable, appropriate, and humane they are. Standards that do not meet the tests of being reasonable, appropriate, and humane are harmful and should be rejected in favor of more humane and better constructed standards. If you let others choose your standards, you will always be subject to the self-serving hypocrisy of authority figures who set up standards that will benefit themselves at the expense of others.

Choose and create appropriate, humane, and reasonable standards for yourself when needed.

Follow your chosen standards and keep a clear conscience. Since the purpose of standards is to help us to gain better outcomes, once you have established appropriate, humane, and reasonable standards for yourself, follow them. If you do not follow well-chosen standards and rules, you will increase the likelihood of failing, being punished, and associating yourself with failure.

Treat yourself well. You have control over whether you create good or bad outcomes for yourself. If you create good outcomes for yourself, your self-esteem will benefit. If you create bad outcomes, your self-esteem will suffer.

Meet your needs acceptably. To ignore your needs or not to exert your full powers toward reasonably meeting your needs will lead to self-hatred and lowered self-esteem.

Be responsible and trustworthy toward yourself. You cannot like or love yourself if you treat yourself irresponsibly and cannot trust yourself to act in your own best interest.

Do what will be best for you and in your best interest, taking into account all of the consequences of your actions for yourself and for others, including all of the long-term and the short-term consequences of your actions. Getting what you want in life will in many instances require giving up your immediate benefit in favor of your long-term benefit, just as it may require sometimes giving up your immediate benefit in favor of the immediate benefit of others.

Stop criticizing and blaming yourself. Chronically criticizing and blaming an OK person is not appropriate, and you are OK!

Treat yourself in a loving and compassionate manner. Be nice to yourself and kind to yourself. Express in your behavior the love that you have for yourself, just as you do toward others you love. Have a compassionate attitude toward yourself.

Comfort yourself. Develop the ability to comfort yourself when you need it, and provide this wonderful gift to yourself. You deserve comforting when you need it.

Take good care of yourself and do good things for yourself, just as you would take good care of someone else whom you liked, loved, or thought well of.

Ensure that you are treated well by others.

Learn to understand others, including their needs, feelings, goals, and motives, so you can predict and influence the behavior of others, get what you need, and help others to get what they need.

Develop effective empathy and other social skills. Empathy is the ingredient most responsible for our ability to get along with each other, and empathy will help you to understand others' perceptions, emotions, and needs, as well as to find the motivation within yourself to develop social contracts that benefit everyone, rather than seeking your own advantage at the expense of others.

Insist on respect from others. Everyone deserves basic respect. In order not to be put in inferior positions and looked down on, you cannot let others disrespect you for inappropriate reasons.

Insist on being treated as fundamentally the equal of others, at all times. Do not accept an inferior position or an unequal share, unless it is based correctly on standards that you have examined and approved.

Learn to express your needs effectively in a social context, and be appropriately assertive regarding your rights and needs. Stand up to those who treat you in demeaning and punishing ways. Assert that you deserve good treatment because you are fundamentally the equal of others and because you are basically a worthwhile and valuable person.

Alter punishing relationships in accord with how you want them to be, including giving up roles and relationships that define you unfairly as being inferior to others or as getting less than others. You have a right to good treatment and a perfect right to ask others to treat you appropriately.

Seek and enjoy new, more supportive, affirming, and gratifying relationships as needed. Relationships that continue to harm you and your self-esteem despite your efforts to change them to be more humane and equitable may need to be abandoned if you are to feel good about yourself. You deserve good treatment from others, and you deserve to choose with whom you will relate in order to get that appropriate, good treatment.

Assert your worth and value in response to cultural and societal attitudes that act against self-esteem by assigning lower worth to certain people on superficial bases, such as age, gender, race, appearance, innate abilities, position, or the simple personal preferences of others. Stand up for the innate equal worth of all people!

Be yourself, with integrity. The epitome of good self-esteem is being yourself joyfully and fully in living your life!

This self-esteem program is complete and covers everything that you will need to understand and do in order to improve your self-esteem (in contrast to some self-help books that give you useful ideas but do not prepare you to deal with all of the barriers that will make it difficult to apply those ideas and create permanent change). Don't feel overwhelmed by the program—it has many parts, but they can all be readily accomplished. If you are willing to work and willing to become a more autonomous person, you can use these ideas to improve your self-esteem significantly! Your "independent mind" will be your chief ally in guiding yourself toward better self-esteem. In fact, it should be clear by now that our attitudes toward ourselves are to a large extent simply a matter of perception, which you can learn to control. You could make your self-esteem positive right now simply by seeing yourself a different way. It is really your choice!

These methods will give you more positive self-esteem, if you apply them with determination and make yourself open to change. You can change your self-esteem, relatively independent of the environment because *your self-esteem feelings are generated inside you—they do not come to you from outside yourself.*

Your self-esteem feelings are generated within you. They do not come directly from outside, so you can be largely in control of them if you choose. You can change your self-esteem by changing your attitudes toward yourself.

Homework: Keep a small notepad with you all the time, and write down the circumstance and what you say every time you criticize or blame yourself. Review your record every night, and notice how silly and meaningless it is to criticize yourself the way you do. Think about how you would rather treat yourself.

Homework: Begin now to express your love for yourself in words or in thoughts at least three times each and every day. Tell yourself that you love you—in the mirror if possible. Enjoy giving yourself this wonderful gift.

Homework: Begin now to do at least one nice thing for yourself each and every day, in order to feel and to demonstrate to yourself your love and caring for yourself. Imagine how good it will feel to do the nice thing for yourself that you have planned for that day, and then carry it out and enjoy!

Chapter Seven

Overcoming Internal Barriers To Change

Progress is impossible without change and those who cannot change their minds cannot change anything.

—George Bernard Shaw

Give Yourself A Break

The basic strategy for improving self-esteem is to change your way of responding to yourself from an unthinking and negative response to a consciously chosen and more positive response.

Right now, you probably don't <u>decide</u> how to feel about yourself or treat yourself—you just do it. To prepare for the process of change, instead of responding automatically, pay attention to how you feel about yourself and treat yourself, and think about whether it makes sense to you and whether it is how you want to be. This means replacing your early childhood self-esteem conditioning with purposive adult conditioning, in which you <u>choose</u> how to respond to yourself more humanely, compassionately, and positively.

Paradoxically, your own resistance to change will be your greatest stumbling block. You will fear change, and you will fear failing if you try to change. You will fear facing the pain of your own poor self-esteem and the reasons for it, and you will fear taking charge of yourself and your self-esteem. You will avoid feeling better about yourself because to do so would be incongruent with what you have always believed—that you deserve to feel bad about yourself. The purpose of this chapter is to make you more aware of these internal barriers to change, and to help you start thinking about how to overcome them in your life.

First, since you have been looking to others to know how to feel about yourself, you must give up depending on them, take control yourself of your self-esteem, and decide for yourself how you feel about yourself. If you are to have stable, positive self-esteem, it must be basically under your control.

You must also give up your own unhealthy methods of trying to compensate for poor self-esteem. If you have tried to feel OK about yourself by acquiring possessions or success or pretending to be better than others, it's time to find your self-esteem within yourself. You are OK just the way you are, and if you reject the inappropriate expectations of others that you have been trying to live up to, and learn to love yourself, you can be OK just within yourself. This also means giving up superficial values that you have held, like believing that people with more money or people who are beautiful are worth more than other people. Looking at people from a more mature viewpoint, people are worthwhile to themselves and to each other because (1) they treat themselves and others decently, (2) they are honest and responsible, with themselves and with others, (3) they support themselves, and (4) they contribute something positive and significant to the lives and welfare of others.

You must be willing to change and willing to see yourself as worthwhile and valuable. Change is frightening, and we want guarantees that if we try something new and different, we will be better off. If you are to make some changes, you must convince yourself that the risk is worth taking—that you believe that you will be better off through making changes than you will be by continuing with what you are already doing. How do you decide whether to proceed into the unknown? Think. Think about your current situation and the self-esteem pain you experience. Think about the problems that your current methods of avoiding that pain are causing you and others, particularly your family. Think about the self-esteem you would like to have and imagine what it would be like. Think about what you would need to do to change. Contemplating all these things will help you decide whether to proceed. (It may also reassure you to enlist someone you think you can trust to serve as a support person while you make these changes.)

In addition to being willing to change, you must be willing to believe that you are valuable. In reality you are the person who now is most valuable to you. You are with yourself more than any other person is with you, you know what feels good to you, and you can do the most to help yourself feel good.

You will need to deal with your own resistance to feeling valuable and to feeling better about yourself—because it is new and unfamiliar, because it contradicts how you have always felt about yourself, and because you are afraid to trust feeling better. If you <u>believe</u> that you deserve to feel OK about yourself, you can get used to these changes. *It is OK to feel good about yourself-even if you are not totally OK.*

It is important that you take responsibility for your self-esteem, and make a commitment to yourself to improve your self-esteem. You are in charge now of shaping your self-concept and self-esteem. Influences on you in your early life may have played a significant role in creating your self-esteem pattern, but now that you are an adult, you cannot sit back and blame those other people and wait (perhaps forever) for them or for anyone else to do something to change your self-esteem for you. You are the one who must do whatever is necessary to improve your self-esteem. No one else "makes" you feel bad about yourself now, unless you allow it to happen.

Being responsible for ourselves is an opportunity not to be under the control of others and an opportunity to use our full powers to do what is truly best for us. You are not responsible <u>to</u> others, but rather you are responsible to yourself.

If you are serious about taking responsibility for your self-esteem, make a commitment to yourself now to improve how you feel about yourself and to do everything that is necessary to accomplish this. This commitment is the crucial beginning step in any process of change.

In order to change, you will need to be honest with yourself about how others have treated you and about how they may have harmed your self-esteem, including those you love. If Dad never spends any time with us, it is easier to explain it as "he works hard and deserves some time for himself" than to recognize that he drinks so much that he can't pay any attention to anyone else. It can be painful to recognize the truth, but it will free you to go ahead and help yourself.

Stop blaming yourself for your poor self-esteem, and give up believing that something about you causes others to treat you badly or to see you as inferior. It seems to be a part of human nature to believe as children that we deserve the treatment that we receive. If we receive rejection and demeanment, then we believe that there is something wrong with us, that we are inferior, and that we should feel bad about ourselves. One of the most important messages in this book is that this is not true. You did not deserve what happened to you that caused your poor self-esteem. Those things were in almost all cases the result of the inability of those around you to do proper parenting or the result of others using you in order to feel better about themselves at your expense!

Consistent with this injunction not to blame yourself, let us say in advance—don't blame yourself if you don't reach your self-esteem goal. If you do your best to apply these methods, but you don't achieve your self-esteem goal, you have not failed. Every person "deserves" positive self-esteem, but you may not be in a position right now to be able to apply the methods fully, because of your level of insecurity, your stress level, etc. Perhaps if you can alter some circumstances, like being under less stress, or being more financially secure, or having a friend to lend some support, it might be just enough to tip the scales the other way and to put you in a position to reach the goal of feeling good about yourself by using these methods. Try seeking additional support from a more psychologically healthy friend, a family member who can be very supportive, your minister, or a therapist or counselor.

Homework—"Imaging" Your Goal
In order to confirm your commitment to better self-esteem, take the next step and imagine your goal. "Imaging" your goal makes the goal more "real" for you, and this enables you to summon up more motivation and persistence for the effort to obtain your goal.

Sit down and relax somewhere where it is quiet and there are no distractions. Close your eyes and concentrate. Allow adequate time—perhaps five to fifteen minutes at a time. Work in the medium that works best for you—that is, if you imagine things in pictures, then do this imaging visually, but if you imagine things best as sounds or feelings, then use those methods. Imagine yourself in your daily life—being at work, doing the housework, talking to friends, going to meetings or church. As you imagine these activities be aware of how you feel in response to yourself. Now, imagine what it would be like to be doing those same activities with positive self-esteem. Let yourself enjoy the difference.

Include in your imaging all the various evidences of self-esteem at the end of Part 1—Chapter Two. Take each of these aspects in turn and imagine yourself feeling or doing it. For example, imagine respecting yourself, how it would feel, in what situations you would like to feel it, and how you would act and feel if you did respect yourself. Imagine saying to yourself, "I respect myself, and it feels good," or "I accept myself for who I am, and it feels good." Imaging the whole list of evidences of self-esteem will take several sessions. You can stop when you are tired, but come back to it until you have created a set of images that cover all aspects of the positive self-esteem that you want to feel. You can use these images on a daily basis, to remind yourself of what you want to achieve.

If you like structure, write out or make a chart of each of the elements of self-esteem, together with the key situations relevant to each in your life, and the new responses you wish to cultivate.

If you have never respected yourself, then naturally it may not be easy to readily imagine respecting yourself. You have known people who you thought respected themselves, however, so imagine yourself feeling what you believe they feel when they feel self-respect or act in self-respecting ways.

Don't give up because imagining yourself feeling good about yourself brings up other feelings that are difficult to tolerate, such as sadness or hurt. When we change anything, it is natural that stored up pain around that issue will come to awareness. If you allow yourself to be fully in touch with these feelings, and stay with them and process them, they will pass eventually. You can take a step forward with your self-esteem right now by comforting yourself and being nice to yourself when you encounter these painful memories. If you simply can't tolerate the feelings that come up, then you can seek help from someone who can help you tolerate them, such as a counselor or therapist.

Don't use inappropriate images. When you imagine perceiving yourself as valuable, don't use an image of acquiring great wealth as equivalent to being valuable. This would be continuing to use the compensations and false values discussed in Part 1—Chapter One!

Start every day with images of the positive self-esteem behaviors you wish for yourself for that day. Prime yourself with these images even before you get out of bed. First read the self-esteem affirmation in Part V - Resource 2, and then imagine how you will implement the affirmations in your actual behavior that day. Make a copy of the affirmation so you can carry it with you and read it for support during the day. Carry a small notebook with you so that you can jot down how you criticize yourself, etc., so that you can consider these things each evening.

Knowing Yourself, Understanding Your Deeper Self, and Being Your Real Self

Two very important barriers to improving self-esteem are ignorance about ourselves and failing to be who we really are. Most people only allow themselves to be aware of the parts of themselves that are positively received by others, and they suppress, deny, and ignore the parts that are not acceptable to others. Since our feelings and thoughts are what tell us what is good for us, if you don't have full access to your feelings and thoughts, you will handicap yourself in your efforts to create good outcomes for yourself. If you don't perceive yourself accurately because you believe uncritically what others tell you about yourself, you are likely to have painful self-esteem feelings that are inappropriate and unnecessary. If you do not know yourself, then you cannot truly love yourself, respect yourself, and accept yourself. (You can only respect, accept, and love the acceptable facade that is all that you acknowledge about yourself.)

Avoiding awareness of aspects of ourselves is very common.Here are some examples. "I don't want to think about my status as a delivery person, since I would then feel ashamed and inadequate for not becoming the owner of the company or an executive, as my parents wanted." We don't want to be in touch with our feelings of poor self-esteem, so we become workaholics and distract ourselves by spending all of our time seeking money and achievements. We don't achieve up to our potential because that would challenge the family view of us as devalued scapegoat, or would make Dad feel bad about his lack of achievement. We don't want to be aware of our hatred for mother because of her emotional abuse, since then we would have to punish ourselves by feeling guilt and shame for having feelings that we are "not supposed to have." (Knowing yourself will mean knowing some things that you don't like about yourself, and this calls on you to accept all of yourself, with all of your scary needs and "inappropriate" thoughts and feelings.)

We have been trained, by society and by our own families, not to be aware of certain emotions and thoughts that we are actually having (most commonly angry and sexual feelings and thoughts, and negative feelings and thoughts about important others). The purpose of this training is to avoid conflict and preserve the social hierarchy. Also, we too often adopt others' inaccurate views and feedback about ourselves, without evaluating them for ourselves.

Work toward knowing yourself fully and accurately by being aware of everything about yourself-all of your thoughts, feelings, needs, wants, motives, and potentials. Don't block your awareness of anything about yourself. We are all human, and we all have our oddities. We all have made mistakes. We all have all kinds of thoughts and feelings, which by themselves do not make us "bad."

There is nothing so bad about you that you can't recognize and understand it. Most of what we are ashamed of or guilty about regarding ourselves is perfectly acceptable, if we were only willing to accept it.

To Know Is Better Than Not To Know.

Get to know yourself. You will find that you are a much more alive, creative, and interesting person than you realized! If certain others can't accept parts of you, then you may choose not to reveal those parts to those other people, but don't hide them from yourself or put yourself down for them.

Once you allow yourself to be fully aware of all aspects of yourself, it becomes possible for you to perceive yourself accurately and realistically. Most of all, this requires using your honest and independent mind to make your own judgments about what is acceptable and appropriate. Your wife may call you "awful," but is it you that is awful, or is it your behavior? And, comparing your behavior with the behaviors of everyone else, is your behavior really "awful," or would it be more reasonable to describe it as "upsetting" or "annoying" to her? It is also important to understand her motives in calling you "awful." Is she reinforcing her self-perception as a martyr, or is she trying to build up guilt in you that she can use later to get you to do something she wants? It is absolutely essential to understand why people say what they say about us, and to demand that the standard to which we are being compared is a reasonable standard.

Be your true self, and don't pretend to be someone else. Every time you believe something false about you that someone else says, and every time you hide things about yourself that you think others would reject, you are pretending to be someone other than who you really are. You might pretend, even to yourself, that you like sports because Dad values sports and hide from yourself the "shameful" truth that you don't like sports at all. The price for this avoidance is that you hate yourself for betraying yourself, and you hate your dad because he won't accept the real you.

Avoiding being yourself leads to self-esteem problems. Every time we distort ourselves in our own eyes or in the eyes of others, we acknowledge that our true self is unacceptable, we hate ourselves for being unacceptable, and we give up the opportunity to associate positive outcomes with our true self and hence give up the opportunity to build solid positive self-esteem.

It is important to understand yourself on a deep level—to use your independent mind and your accurate awareness of yourself to perceive and understand your motives and patterns of behavior, so that you can choose wisely those long-term courses of action that will be best for you, such as choices of career (are you a thinker who will not ultimately be happy in a social occupation, or a conformer who will not be happy in a creative occupation?), marital partner (are you a social person who should not marry a thinker?), and lifestyle (are you a person who needs stable, strong family ties and therefore should not be in a career that takes you away from home a lot?).

The primary barrier to understanding ourselves is not wanting to know the truth about ourselves when the truth is painful. Over and over again, we distort the truth about ourselves because we fear the consequences of being ourselves. For example, we know that we are not intellectually capable of completing college, but we pretend that we are brighter and go anyway because we feel that our parents will only accept us that way. The solution is to see ourselves accurately and know ourselves completely, and then to accept and love who we really are.

Being truthful about ourselves with ourselves means that we cannot lie to ourselves in order to justify harming others in order to get something we want (it's for her own good; it's just business; they deserve it; it's a dog-eat-dog world; they are inferior; etc.) Distorting the truth so we can misuse others for our own short-term advantage results in others perceiving us as being out for our own gain regardless of whether it hurts them. Naturally they will not trust or respect us, and they may be tempted by our behavior to do the same to us.

Even if we try to lie to ourselves about our motives, we can't feel good about ourselves if we are knowingly harming others or treating others by different rules than we apply to ourselves, because of our built-in empathy with the feelings of the people we mistreat and because we ourselves want to be treated nicely by others. It is impossible to completely hide our motives and our harmful behavior from our own deeper awareness, even if we can hide it from our conscious awareness. You know when you are violating what you believe in, and you know when you are harming others, even if you try to hide it from yourself.

If you want to be able to know and understand yourself and others, and if you want to be able to stop pretending and lying to yourself, then make a commitment now to the truth. It may be painful to face reality at first, but the process will set you free! Your independent mind can see, understand, and accept everything about you. You can start by being aware of everything that comes to your senses, and questioning yourself about self-awareness that you think you should have but that seems like a blank spot in your awareness. Things that others seem to know or be in touch with about themselves that you are not aware of and impressions that others have about you that you don't understand are good clues to things that you may have been hiding from yourself. Use your independent mind to know the whole truth about yourself, others, and the world.

PART TWO

THE 12 STEPS TO POSITIVE
SELF-ESTEEM

Step 1

Declare Independence for Your Mind

I was raised to sense what someone wanted me to be and be that kind of person. It took me a long time not to judge myself through someone else's eyes."

—Sally Field

It is absolutely essential in order to have stable, healthy self-esteem that you make your own mind independent of what others say or believe, since all of the various elements of the self-esteem program depend to some degree on using your independent mind.

Letting Others Define Who You Are and Determine Your Basic Worth

It is natural for children and adults to be affected by what others think of them and feel about them, but you cannot allow your self-esteem to be primarily controlled by what others think and feel about you and still have good self-esteem. We do need to know how others are reacting to us and why, but we must be able to take in the useful information in how others react to us, while reserving for ourselves the final judgment about ourselves and our behavior. This means developing your own independent view of yourself and others, against which you can evaluate the reactions of others.

If someone says "You're awful," or "You hurt me," you cannot allow yourself to automatically feel bad or feel bad about yourself, because that puts your self-esteem and your understanding of reality in the control of others. You must first evaluate the truth and reasonableness of others' statements. Then you can decide how you really feel and how you want to respond. Even if your mother says "You are worthless," you should train yourself not to simply and automatically feel bad about yourself or define yourself as a bad person or a failure, without examining why she said this and what she really means.

You must realize that another person's words and feelings express his or her individual and idiosyncratic (even sometimes peculiar) view of the world and his or her emotional responses to the world (and to you as part of that world). There isn't anything automatically true or false about anyone's perceptions and feelings. In fact, people have radically different views and feelings about things, and no one person or group has the complete truth. What your parents think and feel about you is not "the truth" about you—it is simply their viewpoint. If you have been unfortunate enough to have experienced many times as a child unrealistically negative views and feelings of others about you, then you may well have damaged self-esteem now because of this, and you will need to go back and re-evaluate all of that input, to see if it was in fact true and realistic, or whether it was biased and unrealistic. If it was biased and unrealistic, then your view of and feelings about yourself should be revised in the light of your new understanding.

You cannot allow another person's reactions to you to totally or automatically determine your self-esteem.

In order to protect your self-esteem, you cannot automatically take what anyone else says about you as the truth.

You must be the guardian of your truth, because it will be the fundamental determinant of how you feel toward yourself.

As a child you were assigned a place in the family and a share of the rewards available. These were communicated by what was said (You are wonderful, You are worthless) and by how each person was treated (such as paying attention to and giving rewards to others but not to you). If your place and your share were basically equal to those of others, then you will tend to feel OK about yourself and basically equal to others. If your place and share were less than those of others, then you will probably feel inferior to them and bad about yourself.

As an adult you must re-evaluate your inferiority, to see whether it was reasonable and how it came to be. Since in almost all cases your inferiority was decided by someone else, based on his or her personal and biased views and feelings, you must now reject that label and assert your equality and your right to an equal share of things in life. Just because your father saw you as inferior does not mean that you were in any way inferior. Perhaps you can't change the fact that he saw you as inferior, but you can change whether you believe that you were in fact inferior.

Allowing Others' Standards and Expectations To Determine Your Self-Esteem

In the same way, if you feel bad about yourself because you are "not good enough" in the eyes of someone else, then you must understand the standard being used for how good you would have to be in order to be good enough! You must understand who set up the standard and why. The standard you think you must live up to is most likely the idiosyncratic product of another individual's personal and biased point of view, and you may need to reject that standard and re-evaluate how you feel about yourself with respect to the behavior in question and how you feel about yourself for being "not good enough" in that person's eyes.

Just because your father says, "You disappoint me," you should not automatically feel bad about yourself, without first understanding why he is disappointed and deciding for yourself whether what he is expecting of you is reasonable or unreasonable. You should first ask enough questions that you understand exactly why he is disappointed and then evaluate for yourself whether you have done something that in your own view justifies feeling bad about yourself. If by disappointed he means that you forgot something he asked you to do, then you can consider how meaningful this was. If you forgot one thing he asked you to do, it might not justify feeling bad about yourself, but if you forget things he asks frequently, then you might feel bad. It's up to you. No one, including your parents, has the right to set standards for you that automatically determine your feelings toward yourself. They can state what they want from you, and they can say what they require from you in order for you to get their love and approval, but you must decide whether not meeting those desires and requirements merits feeling bad toward yourself. If these requirements are unrealistic or harmful to you, then you may be better off looking for love, support, and approval elsewhere—from yourself and from other available sources.

It is painful and sad to realize that you may never meet your parents' standards and expectations, and that you may never be able to get the love you wanted from your parents, but that does not mean that you are inferior or that you should feel bad about yourself. You may feel sad because you cannot please them and get their approval, but if you are to have good self-esteem, you cannot let that make you feel bad about yourself.

Changing Your Mind About Your Responsibility for Others' Feelings

One of the traps that keeps us from having our own independent minds is feeling responsible for the feelings of others when those others blame us for their pain. Your mother, for example, might blame you for her unhappy life, and if you feel bad about yourself when she says that, then you are accepting her version of reality, and you will find it difficult to consider for yourself whether or not you have some responsibility in the matter. It is important to think this through for yourself.

You are not responsible for others' pain if you have acted reasonably and appropriately toward them and have not knowingly tried to harm him. Just because your mother feels bad and blames it on having to take care of you does not mean that you did anything wrong or that you should feel bad at all. You did not cause her problem. As an adult it is her responsibility to care for her child, and that is her problem. The child is not responsible for this. If your father says "I feel upset every time I'm around you," then you must understand why he feels that way. If you have acted appropriately and reasonably toward him, then his upset is "caused" by him (by his unusual reactions to things) and not by you. You may feel sad for them or sorry for them, and you may feel sad that you cannot please them, but that should not lead you to criticize, reject, or feel bad about yourself.

If you are to have good self-esteem, you cannot let others control your self-esteem by blaming you when things are not your fault.

Criticizing and Rejecting Yourself

We learned habits of criticizing and rejecting ourselves from parents who were unhappy with us, and this is another area in which you must assert your right to judge for yourself.

You reject yourself (the opposite of acceptance) every time you think that something about you is not OK or not adequate.

The most common and hurtful self-criticisms are telling yourself that you are stupid, dumb, crazy, lazy, worthless, unlovable, no good, not good enough, a failure, that you don't deserve any better, and that you will never succeed or amount to anything. (How often do you tell yourself things like these?) Every time you tell yourself these things, you strengthen the connection in your mind between yourself (as the "cause" of this negative feedback) and bad outcomes for yourself (the pain of hearing these things about yourself). The more you tell yourself these inappropriate, negative things, the worse you will feel about yourself. (At times there may be something about you that you wish to change, but you do not have to label it as bad, not OK, or inadequate in order to change it.)

Criticizing and rejecting yourself is the primary thing now maintaining your poor self-esteem. In order to have good self-esteem, you must not accept the criticisms or rejections of others (or of yourself) as being justified without deciding for yourself whether they are justified. You must insist on using your independent mind to make your own judgment, and you must question and examine your own criticisms and rejections just as much as those coming from others.

Developing and Using Your Independent Mind

You can counteract the effects of others' mistreatment and rejections and the effects of your own mistreatment and rejection of yourself by using your independent mind. (1) You can know with certainty that what others feel or say about you is only their individual viewpoint, thereby gaining more control over when and why you feel bad about yourself. (2) You can recognize how others put you in inferior positions and give you unequal shares, and you can refuse to accept this as what you deserve in life. You can learn to insist on equal respect and an equal share in life. (3) You can question standards others apply to you and realize that these standards and expectations are once again only the personal opinions of other individuals. You can see yourself as OK even if you aren't "enough" in the eyes of your parents or certain others. You can choose for yourself more humane and reasonable standards for yourself. (4) You can recognize how you take responsibility inappropriately for others' feelings and blame yourself if they feel bad (regardless of your contribution), and you can reject this responsibility, letting them bear the responsibility for their own decisions, feelings, and lives. (5) You can use your independent mind to recognize the unreasonableness of your self-criticisms and the hurtful destructiveness of your self-rejection. You can stop doing these things and learn to treat yourself in a more loving and compassionate way!

It is particularly exciting to note that since self-esteem is determined by your perceptions of yourself, you can use your independent mind to take control of your self-esteem! Self-esteem happens inside you and is not determined outside of you or outside of your control! Your perceptions of yourself are opinions and feelings, not facts that can be proven or disproven. You can make your perceptions of yourself positive, or at least more positive, by yourself. No one has to do it for you. You don't have to prove anything to anyone else in order to perceive yourself positively. You can see yourself positively even if others don't. For example, if your family does not believe that your needs are as important as those of others in the family, they may dispute your assertion of equal rights or forcibly deny you an equal share, but you can still believe that you deserve equal treatment, and you can disagree with them and assert your right to feel good about yourself! It's up to you. If you have believed that you are inferior to others, you can decide to believe the opposite!

If it is as simple as changing your mind, why isn't this easy to do? The main reason is habit—that you have assumed for years that it is "true" about you that you are inferior. Now you can use your independent mind to <u>reconsider</u> your assumption. If you were not inferior to start with (because your inferiority was assigned to you inappropriately by someone else), then there is no reason to continue to believe or feel that you are inferior. You can now think back to those times when you were given messages that you were inferior and view them in a new light-that you were not inferior even though you were being treated as inferior. The fact that people treated you as inferior doesn't mean that you deserved it or that you were in any sense inferior. This fresh understanding of the situation will revolutionize your life!

Another reason that people do not adopt more healthy beliefs is that to do so threatens those who do not agree and may lead to conflict. If your family has used you as a dumping ground for their frustrations by using you as a scapegoat or by treating you any way they wanted to, and you begin to tell them that they are wrong to do so, or you fight back, they will not like it, and they will either adjust to your new efforts, or they will try even harder to keep you in that inferior role. You must persevere with your new assertions and not give in. No one has the right to treat you unfairly, and you do not deserve unfair treatment just for being yourself.

Having your own independent mind is a form of self-assertion in that you assert your right to see the truth and your right to have your own beliefs and feelings, apart from what others want you to believe or feel. You will like yourself and respect yourself for asserting these rights!

Step 2

You Have Basic Value
Independent of Others

What you think about yourself is much more important than what others think of you.

—Seneca

You have fundamental worth and value as a person, independent of how others treat you. You are not defined fundamentally by others' reactions to you or by what they say about you, and your value is not the same as the value that others place on you.

As young children, our sense of self and self-value are determined almost entirely by how we interpret how our families treat us. We see ourselves through the eyes of our families. Many people never mature beyond this way of determining their identity and value—never seeing that there is more to them than the reactions of others to them. The critical problem with this is that our self-esteem is then determined by how others react to us, which makes us slaves to the value that others place on us. If your only value is in how others value you, then others can get you to do almost anything they want by expressing displeasure toward you. Your self-esteem is under their control, and you can be manipulated (blackmailed) at will. The goal of this book is to help you to be more (though not totally) independent of external events and of the reactions of others to you.

When others are unhappy with you, do you think "I must be terrible," "I must be a terrible person," "What did I do wrong?", "It's awful that they are unhappy with me," or "What's wrong with me that I can't please anyone?"? If so, then you need to change your way of valuing yourself, from "I'm only valuable if someone else thinks I am valuable" to "I have innate and fundamental value as a person, and I'm valuable to myself as well, regardless of how others see me, although I may be sad about it or have more difficulty getting what I want in the world if no one else values me."

The first basic distortion in thinking that maintains dependence on others for your value is the belief that you should be like everyone else. Most people are only comfortable with people like themselves, so if you are desperate to please others (because that is the only way you believe that you have value), then you will try to be just like others so that you won't offend them. You will exist only for other people and not as yourself. We have noted that it is necessary for societal purposes that we get along with our fellow human beings and conform to certain standards of behavior (how we treat others, what language we use, how we behave). Beyond that, however, is a vast area of experience and thought in which you are free to be yourself, for yourself. If you exist only for purposes of pleasing others or fitting in with others, then you are neglecting most of what you could be as a person, since you could be so much more. Work on becoming a separate person, existing in your own right, with as much right to be yourself as others have.

The second basic distortion in thinking that maintains your dependence on others for your value is ignoring value that you have aside from how others value you. If you only have value to others, then you are ignoring your value to yourself, including your ability to produce for yourself the outcomes you want. As adults it matters much more how we treat ourselves than what we get from others.

We are with ourselves every second of every day of our existence, and as adults the reactions we have to ourselves and how we treat ourselves in each moment have a much greater impact on our welfare and our quality of life than how others treat us (as important as that may be). You must come to fully appreciate your value to yourself, which will help you to put in better perspective the value that you have to others.

The third distortion of thinking that maintains your dependence on others for your value is "it is crucial that certain other people have positive reactions to me, and if they don't, then I should feel bad in response to myself until they do." The fact is that you can survive, prosper, and be happy, regardless of whether certain other important persons (father, mother, current spouse, boss, etc.) are reacting positively to you. Regardless of whether certain others react positively to you, a reasonable outside observer could very well conclude that you were OK. You are the one making it so crucial to have their approval, and you can give up having to have their approval. If you do, you may have to find other things to do with your time, like doing things that please you and are good for you!

You may feel sad about giving up trying to please others and get your value from them. It's OK to feel sad about this, but it is better that you give it up and feel sad about it for a while than to continue to base your self-esteem mainly on the reactions of others. This does not mean that you won't care how people feel about you. You will still care, but you will consider how to think and feel in response to the displeasure and criticism of others, rather than automatically feeling bad the way you used to.

Homework: Every morning before you get up, think to yourself "I am my own person—I am valuable and worthwhile to myself even if others don't value me right now. I want to have positive relationships with others today, but I will still be OK even if others are displeased or do not approve."

(See the end of Part I—Chapter Five for a discussion of doing what is best for oneself versus doing what is best for the group.)

Step 3

You Are Basically Equal To
and Not Inferior to Others

Doubt whom you will, but never doubt yourself.
—Christian Nestal Bovee

You are fundamentally the equal of others, and you have the right to expect equal treatment from others. No one has the right to make you inferior or to reduce what should be your equal share solely on the basis of his or her feelings or personal preferences.

Our attitudes about whether we are equal to others are established in childhood by how we are treated compared to others. If a parent gives a child a lesser share (of food, toys, love, etc.) than that received by other family members (especially other children in the family), the child interprets this to mean that he is not as deserving or worthwhile as those who get more. The child therefore perceives himself as inferior, feels inferior, and adopts the stance and identity of one who is inferior, and the child's self-esteem is impaired. This will also occur when parents make their own needs routinely more important than the child's needs or when the child serves as a family scapegoat.

Being fundamentally equal to others does not, of course, imply that we are identical to others. Every individual is unique, but we are equal to others in terms of certain fundamental rights and in the ways that we should be treated by our fellow human beings. Every person has the right to be treated equally with respect to rules and laws that apply to everyone of the same group (whether that is in the family, the school room, the work place, or society in general); and every person has equal right to the conditions that make for positive self-esteem (such as your right to exist, your right to be yourself, being treated as an equal to others who are like you in the group, and the right to be treated with the same respect that others in the group receive).

Status Hierarchies, Power, Superiority, and Inferiority

Human beings who are dominant over others get a larger share of the available goods than those they dominate. Efforts to sort out who is dominant could lead to constant conflicts and killings, so in order to stabilize these power arrangements, we create status hierarchies to define what share of the available goods each of us deserves. People therefore strive to be above others in the status hierarchy in order to get more of what they want.

Those who get a larger share typically feel superior to and more highly deserving than those lower on the hierarchy, simply because they get a larger share. (This derives from our childish reasoning that those who get more must deserve more and those who get less must be less deserving.) People may also strive to be higher in the hierarchy simply to feel superior and thereby bolster shaky self-esteem.

Superiority and status inevitably damage the self-esteem of those placed in inferior (lower) positions. If some are superior, then inevitably others will be inferior. If some are winners in competition, then others will be losers. If you become superior (better than others, more deserving than others in your family, or higher in community status), then those who are lower than you will end up with worse self-esteem, since people in inferior positions naturally attribute lesser value to themselves because they receive less of the available rewards. This effect is enhanced if those in superior positions show contempt or demeaning attitudes toward them. If our striving for more is tied in our minds to being better than others, then it becomes even more destructive to the self-esteem of those others (socially destructive self-esteem).

Our individualistic, competitive society is a perfect setting for people to demonstrate superiority over others, by winning, having more money, a better job, a better education, a better car, etc. Many in our society have some awareness of the silliness and immaturity of this striving for superiority through consumer goods. The bumper sticker "He who dies with the most toys, wins" pokes fun at our foolishness (although it does not suggest that we stop it).

Achieving superiority over others is only a temporary fix, of course, since being in a superior status is vulnerable to the efforts of others to unseat us. We could lose our superiority at any time (and almost certainly will lose it as we become elderly, if not sooner).

Equality is not the most natural state for human societies, as we can see from human history. The first state of human societies is rule by power and the subjugation of other human beings to our own interests. None of us is above such attitudes. Many perfectly upstanding, moral citizens two hundred years ago believed that it was perfectly OK to enslave other human beings, and that this was OK in the eyes of God as well. The historical subjugation of women is another example of our willingness for the strong to take what they can from others, and to use whatever rationalizations they can to make it seem justified. The typical rationalization is that those who are subjugated are in fact inherently inferior (Blacks are inferior to whites, women are inferior to men, etc.), and that their inferior positions are therefore appropriate or deserved.

The long history of struggles for human rights demonstrates that those who are made inferior do not rest until the inferiority is righted. They will never fully accept the imposed inferiority, regardless of others' rationalizations that they deserve it. In families, for instance, children who are made inferior fight back by striving to become superior to their siblings or by passive-aggressive methods-being stubborn and uncooperative and making mistakes on purpose to inconvenience those who are superior. Achieving superiority may help the individual temporarily, but it is no overall solution to the societal problem because it simply perpetuates the pattern of some being superior and some being inferior.

Since a situation of forced inequality is fundamentally unstable, since people will continue to strive to achieve equality until they reach it, and since fundamental equality is more fair than inequality, perhaps equality should be our choice of a social ethic from the start. It is my personal belief that superiority-inferiority systems, including our own society, have a basically immoral quality, partly because they reliably establish negative self-esteem in those who are inferior. I believe that it would be a much better world if we gave up striving for superiority completely and turned our attention to accepting ourselves as we are and enjoying the fruits of being who we are (without comparing ourselves with others).

Inferiority and status inevitably damage self-esteem. Only basic equality can remove superiority as a threat to self-esteem.

"Win-Win" Solutions Lead to Greater Equality

The world could be a much different place if we all believed that we would get more by helping everyone benefit from any given transaction than we would get by trying to win and get more than others. The fact that the world is the way it is indicates that most people still believe that they can get more by looking for opportunities to take from others and to be superior to others.

Do you believe that you can get more by always trying to get as much as you can, regardless of the outcomes for others, or do you believe that you can get more in the long run by ensuring that others "win" as well as you? Why do you believe that? How things are is not the only way they can be. Are you willing to try more cooperative, "win-win" solutions?

We need a respected societal ethic that reinforces a more mature, cooperative stance toward relationships. Our churches, being by and large strongly committed to the status quo and highly avoidant of internal conflict, have status hierarchies within themselves and have not provided us with much leadership in this regard. We must come to respect strength more than power, benevolence more than domination, cooperation more than winning, success more than superiority, responsibility more than opportunism, and empathy more than manipulation. It is my contention that those who have high total self-esteem (true_self_-esteem, which is relatively independent of what others think of them) do not need to dominate or win over others and tend to be more understanding and compassionate people than those with low self-esteem and those who try to compensate for low self-esteem with evaluative self-esteem strivings.

You can get more in life by appropriately balancing your needs with those of others than you can by taking whatever you can get regardless of how it affects others.

Everyone Deserves Equal Treatment

You deserve equal treatment with regard to the rules that apply to everyone in your status in any particular group. As a member of the group of "citizens" you should have an equal right with all other "citizens" to vote, equal protection under the laws, etc. As a member of your family, you should have equal respect and be accorded equal basic worth by the other family members. In general, you have the right to be treated equally with the other members within the group at issue.

Equality does not mean that we should all get exactly the same things in life. We are not identical to each other as individuals, and our circumstances are all different. You should not necessarily get the same number of toys as the children in some other family, but you should share in your own family's wealth equally with the other children in your family. You should have equal opportunity to work, but if you choose not to work, then you have no right to expect others to supply you with an income equal to that of those who do work.

Children provide an example of different rights for different groups based on context. Children have the same basic worth as persons as adults and should receive the same basic respect as adults. However, because of their dependent and less able status, children have different privileges and responsibilities. Children do not have the right to drink alcohol, for example, and they are not expected to work and support themselves. Within a family, the rights of children will vary somewhat with their age grouping, due to age differences in maturity and responsibility (although every child in the family should still be treated with the same basic respect).

Everyone Deserves Equal Respect

To treat someone with respect means to act as if the person were worthy of high regard, to avoid interfering with that person's legitimate efforts to meet his needs, and to avoid violating that person's rights. Our society says that every person is entitled to be treated with the same basic respect as every other person regardless of differences such as age, gender, race, sexual orientation, religion, or handicap. I believe the same basic respect is also due to everyone regardless of appearance, achievements, wealth, or social standing. (If you want to admire someone because of his appearance, achievements, wealth, social standing, or anything else, you may do that, but you should not respect him more than anyone else.)

The special relevance of respect to equality and self-esteem is that to be disrespected or treated with lack of respect usually leads to feelings of shame and inferiority, which are prime enemies of self-esteem. Parents often try to train children to obey by purposely treating them with disrespect in order to induce these shame and inferiority feelings. To treat everyone with basic respect at all times, then, would be a move toward guaranteeing everyone a chance at good self-esteem.

In addition, everyone should be <u>treated</u> with the same basic respect even if we do not actually feel the same respect for him or her. Thus, we should treat criminals and those who have injured us with that same basic respect, even though we dislike them or wish them harm. It helps the civility of our society and the self-esteem of everyone if we always treat everyone with that same basic respect (treating them as if they were worthy of high regard and/or esteem). This is not hypocritical-it is simply a choice of whether to use disrespect as a punishment. It is never necessary to use disrespect as a punishment, even when one has lost the feeling of respect for someone. It is just as effective a strategy-and more humane-to tell the person directly that one has lost respect for her, and to apply other reinforcements, while continuing to treat the person with the same basic respect. You can be angry with someone and at the same time treat that person with basic respect.

Everyone Has Equal Basic Worth

We are all equally valuable in terms of our basic worth as persons. Your parents might be more important to you than anyone else in the world, but you should not confuse their value to you with their basic worth as persons. The fact that they are valuable to you does not make them better than or more valuable than anyone else in the world, in terms of their basic worth as persons. The President is no better than any of the rest of us and deserves no more respect than the town cripple does, even though the President is performing a very important function and may deserve certain protections or higher pay or the deference of others because of that. We should remember that the personal importance that we ascribe to others, because of their position, fame, or relationship to us, are added in our minds on top of the basic equal worth that all people have. This issue is of critical importance for your self-esteem, because if you perceive important persons as having greater basic worth than you, then you are inferior to them, and this will be a self-esteem problem for you.

Your Needs Are Just As Important As Those of Others

Since you are basically equal to others, your needs are just as important as those of others, and you have just as much right as others to the good things available in life to all. If you believe that others' needs are more important than yours, you will naturally see yourself as inferior to them, and your self-esteem will be lowered. Having your needs be more important than those of others might seem better than having them be less important than others' needs, but it is not a good solution overall, since this will lead to inferiority for someone else, as well as perpetuating the struggle for superiority. The socially desirable and socially stable answer must lie in some form of equality. Your needs must be as important as those of others-not more important and not less important.

Some might argue that a child's needs are more important than his parents' needs, but this in an illusion. A parent may leave something she enjoys doing to take care of her child's need of the moment, but that is not because the child's need is more important-it is because it is more important to the mother at that moment to meet the child's need than to continue attending to her own. Of course, the mother's needs for survival and health must be met even if it involves not meeting some of the child's needs, because if the mother's survival and health needs are not met, the child will be without a caretaker!

Some would claim that it is a good thing to sacrifice one's own needs for others' needs, but an unflinchingly objective view of human behavior reveals that we always do what we believe to be in our best interest, even when we seem to be sacrificing our lives for someone else's! Sacrifices that are made freely, therefore, are gifts and not sacrifices, and sacrifices that are made with strings attached are covert transactions that lead to lots of trouble later.

It can be complicated to figure out how to make your needs and those of others equal. If a family has limited resources, and one child wants to go to college, and the other child wants a loan from the family to start a business, which will the family do if it cannot do both? Clearly this will take some discussion, maneuvering, and soul-searching for the family. They might decide to divide what help they can give evenly, even though it is not enough to meet either need adequately. They might decide to pay for college for the one child, who then promises to invest a certain amount of money in the other child's business. There are many ways to make both needs equally important. The important thing is that it be worked out so that both children feel equally valued and loved.

Feeling Equal To Others

The principal barrier to feeling equal to others is usually that you feel undeserving or less deserving of respect and equal treatment than others. This sense of what we deserve as persons is a part of our self-concept or identity, and usually we hold onto a stable identity as part of our security in the world, even if it results in pain for us. In order to feel good about yourself it is essential to feel as deserving as others, and the best way to feel more deserving is to change your mind about it-to re-evaluate the experiences that caused you to feel less deserving and decide that you were not in fact less deserving but that you simply accepted that inferior role for yourself.

Identify how you were treated that led you to believe that you were not equal or equally deserving as others. Change your mind about this experience. The fact that your parents gave you a smaller share or loved you less than others did not mean that you deserved less or that you were not basically equal to others. If you felt inferior because your father heavily favored your brother and frequently demeaned you, then you must understand now that you were actually just as good as your brother, and that your father's attitude was his own personal preference and meant nothing about you. You must come to understand that your conclusion about being inferior and undeserving was wrong, even though it may have helped you to make the best of a situation that you could not change at the time. Decide now that you were (and are) in fact basically equal and just as deserving as everyone else.

After changing your mind on this point, accept that it is OK for you to receive good things-that it is consistent with your new sense of identity to deserve whatever good things are available. Next, you can change your interactions with others to reflect your equal status. Identify the circumstances in which you currently let your needs be less important than those of others. Who are the people who tend to put your needs lower, and why are they doing this? What do you need to do to change your mind and adopt a more healthy attitude about your own needs? Every night, review the day and examine those instances in which you allowed others' needs to be more important than yours. Get clear on why you allowed it, sympathize with yourself for the pain it caused you, forgive yourself, and imagine a similar circumstance and how you will act differently next time.

Imagine and practice in fantasy asserting your right to an equal share. You might say, "I know that in the past I have usually taken a smaller share [or a lesser role, or less credit, or a smaller piece of pie, or whatever], but that has not been fair to me, and it's time that I get the same as everyone else." Anticipate the complaints of others about this change. Those who have benefited from your inferiority (by getting a larger share themselves) may complain now if you try to get an equal share, but they have no rightful basis for complaining. You have the right to basic equality. Practice what you will say to them if they complain, such as " I realize that this means a change for you, but the old way was just not right, and it was certainly not fair to me, and I am determined to change it." Imagine the conversation until you know that you can reply assertively no matter what they say.

After you are relatively comfortable with what you will say to assert yourself and to reply to those who complain, use these new thoughts and assertions in actual situations. You may be scared at first, but do it anyway, and keep doing it. You will like yourself for standing up for yourself, even if you are scared. You cannot force others to treat you as an equal, but you must at least speak up, voicing your complaint and identifying the inequality as unfair and inappropriate. In the past, when you were put down for asserting your needs, you would feel ashamed and confirmed in your inferiority. Now, you will feel and act equal, so that when others try to put you down, you will feel like an equal who is being denied the equal treatment you rightly deserve. You may feel insulted or angry, but you will not feel ashamed or inferior any longer, because their view of you no longer controls how you see yourself!

If you express your needs for equality, and others refuse to change, then you will need to seek relationships with new people who are willing to see you as equal and treat you as equal. Make a promise to yourself never to go back to the old inferiority. *You are basically equal to others and just as deserving as anyone else.*

Step 4

You Did Not Deserve to be Treated Badly

If rejection destroys your self-esteem, you're letting others hold you as an emotional hostage.

—Brian Tracy

We all received some treatment in our early caretaking that we interpreted to mean that there was something wrong with us and that we did not deserve to feel any better or be treated any better. Even if our parents were very good at caretaking, the simple fact that we had to adjust to doing things in prescribed ways-like eating at certain times in certain ways, eliminating only in certain places, and speaking only in the words of our parents' language-guaranteed that we would feel that our own natural ways of doing things were not acceptable (and therefore that certain aspects of ourselves were not acceptable).

If these normal disappointments are the worst that we experience, then like most people, we will be somewhat uncertain about our acceptability and careful to conform and to please others as needed, but if we receive harmful, hostile caretaking or are made in other ways to feel inferior to other family members, then we will have much more serious problems with our self-esteem.

It is a curious fact about human beings that we tend to believe that how we are treated is how we should be treated and that what we get is what we deserve, especially if this is stated or encouraged by our caretakers. Children who are abused frequently twist the facts around to believe that they caused or deserved the abuse, just as children whose parents divorce quite regularly suspect that they caused the divorce. Children simply don't know any better, or they inappropriately take responsibility for inappropriate parental behaviors so as not to provoke even worse treatment. It is very important to correct these false beliefs.

Bad treatment or abuse that you received was almost certainly the result of your parents' failures or personal problems and was not directly your fault. Children often hear the exact opposite from parents"If you would be good, I wouldn't have to punish you," "The devil's in you, and I have to beat it out," or even "You made me hit you." These messages tell us that it is our fault that we are punished or mistreated. Messages about our worthlessness, such as "You're no good" and "You don't deserve to be in this family" reinforce our undeservingness as well. *You almost certainly did not cause or deserve treatment you received that was seriously injurious to your self-esteem.*

It is necessary, of course, that we learn what the consequences of our various behaviors are, but this learning is usually not injurious to self-esteem, as long as the consequences we receive are commensurate with and appropriate to our behavior. When the consequences are unnecessarily harsh or inappropriate, they can do lasting damage to self-esteem. I believe that as adults we can all distinguish the appropriate consequences (spanking, verbal correction, getting stung by a bee we are playing with) from the inappropriate consequences (being beaten, receiving a tongue-lashing, our parent putting a bee on us to sting us again so we won't ever get near a bee again). You were not responsible for the <u>inappropriate</u> consequences, punishments, corrections, or abuse that you received.

It is important that you allow yourself to know the truth about how you were treated. This requires knowing what was appropriate treatment and what was not, but as noted above, as adults we all do know what was appropriate and what was not, if we allow ourselves to know. Children need their parents, can be seriously hurt by their parents, and are not in a position to rebel effectively, so they often need to fool themselves about their parents' mistreatment, but as adults it is OK for us to know the truth. It is OK for you to see the truth about how you were treated.

The benefit of seeing the truth is that you can stop blaming and punishing yourself for things that were the responsibility of others. This will allow you to relax about yourself and to feel like a really OK person. The difficulty with seeing the truth is that you may feel considerable emotional pain about how you were treated (since you are no longer blaming yourself), and your relationship with your parent may be threatened. You may be angry, and you may want your parents to acknowledge what they did or to apologize. It's OK to be self-protectively and self-supportively angry, since you need your own affirmation and support. Your anger need not result in you harming anyone. Just let yourself be angry, and let the anger run its course. As you stop feeling inappropriately responsible yourself and as you feel more confident that you will not let yourself be mistreated again, your anger will diminish.

It is uncertain whether you can get acknowledgment or an apology from others for what they did to you in the past. A few people can acknowledge how they have harmed others and be sorry about it, but many people will be too defensive to admit what they may in fact now be sorry for, because they fear the guilt or other consequences of doing so.

You may also be angry with yourself for allowing the bad treatment, even if you acknowledge that you did not cause it in the first place. You will need to be realistic about whether you could have effectively avoided the bad treatment. Children are often not in a position to resist effectively or to avoid what adults do to them. If you assess the situation realistically and still believe that you could have and should have done more to protect yourself, then you must accept that you harmed yourself, and you must forgive yourself for not taking better care of yourself. This involves accepting our imperfections and failures, yet being able to see our value and worth at the same time. (See the discussion in Step 7 on accepting yourself for detailed instructions on forgiving yourself.)

The essential thing for you now is to understand and accept that you did not cause the bad treatment, and to free yourself from self-blame, so that you can joyfully use your full energies to make good things happen for yourself in life.

Step 5

You Have the Right to Exist
and to Be Yourself

What's a man's first duty? The answer is brief: To be himself.
                                                        —Henrik Ibsen

It is impossible to have good self-esteem if you do not believe that you have the right even to exist in this world. Doubting your right to exist usually derives from hearing messages from parents that you are not wanted, that they wish you had not been born, or that they wish you would go away or disappear. Sometimes these parents openly blame a child for all of the parents' problems, since the child is a convenient person to blame. Children who come to believe that they should not exist may try to kill themselves, become "accident prone"— unconsciously causing frequent harm to themselves, or punish themselves in other ways. They are also depressed, which we can readily understand!

If a person believes that she does not have the right to exist, it is because she has made the negative feelings and views of someone else about her (that she is not wanted or that it is hoped that she will disappear) into her own self-definition. The fact that your parents did not want you to exist <u>does not mean</u> that you are not supposed to exist or that you do not have the right to exist. It means only that your parents did not want you to exist. They do not have the power or the right to determine whether you should exist.

Everyone has the right to exist, and this includes you. This right is not earned; you have it simply because you are alive.

In order to regain your right to exist, don't allow others' negative views of you to define you. Some people try to explain why their parents did not want them by finding things wrong with themselves, believing that if they had been better, their parents would have wanted them. Parents may express specific reasons for their displeasure—

"you're not smart enough,"

"you're not athletic enough,"

"you're not pretty enough,"

"you're a boy and I wanted a girl,"

"you're a girl and I wanted a boy,"

"I didn't want any children at all," etc., but usually the true reason is that the parent cannot love and give to anyone. All children deserve the right to exist and deserve basic acceptance and love, without having to earn these things.

You must face the fact that your parents did not want you to exist, reject your parents' wish that you not exist, and demand for yourself and give yourself the right to exist. You can use your independent mind to help yourself understand clearly that your existence and your rights are not determined by your parents or by anyone else and that you have a right to exist regardless of whether your parents wanted you. Everyone is good enough to exist, and everyone has a perfect right to exist. You did not lack any qualities that would have made you lovable and acceptable. You did not "fail." Your parents failed you. If they could not give you love, acceptance, and the basic right to exist, then nothing you could have done would have changed that. They did not give you these responses because they could not give them. The problem was within them-they could not bear their own pain in living, and they blamed you to make themselves feel better. You were OK the way you were.

Blaming yourself for your parents' rejection may seem easier to you than acknowledging that they failed you and therefore being angry at them, but blaming yourself has destroyed your self-esteem. Most other parents could have accepted you—you were just unlucky to end up in the family you had.

It is paradoxical that people who do not give themselves the right to exist because they were not acceptable to their parents almost always think that others in the same situation do have a right to exist. They can perceive the right of other children to exist, regardless of parental rejection, but they do not extend the same right to themselves! If anyone has the right to exist, then you, too, have the right to exist-you are no different. Every child has the right to exist!

People whose right to exist has been denied by parents often feel that the only way their right to exist can be restored is for those same parents to give it back to them, so they try for years to please and change those parents. This is usually a fruitless effort, since parents who have denied a child's right to exist are very unlikely later to soften and become more loving and giving. As long as one continues to try to be better or to change one's parents, one does not have to face the feelings of despair, rejection, hurt, and failure that may well result from finally accepting that one's parents are never going to give one what one needs. Nevertheless, accepting this reality is the only way to move on, and you must move on, believing that you are valuable and that you have a perfect right to exist. The choice is up to you—you can continue to believe your parents' negative estimations of you and continue to feel bad about yourself, or you can rebel by refusing to take their estimations of you as the truth about you and by developing your own independent view of and feelings about yourself.

If you "feel" that you should harm or kill yourself because your parents did not want you or wanted you gone, the solution, paradoxically, is not to become what your parents would approve of but to become more truly yourself! Your unnatural notion that you should be harmed or dead was adopted from someone else who had those feelings or thoughts, and you are carrying out those thoughts, like a robot. The solution is to reject those thoughts and arrive at your own feelings and beliefs about yourself. You must develop your independent mind. You and every other person have the right to exist. It is time for you to claim that right.

You Have the Right to Be Yourself

Not only do you have the right to exist, but you also have the right to be yourself, and so does every other person, with the single requirement that you do not harm others by being yourself. It is the greatest pleasure in life to be fully and joyfully yourself, and being yourself is an important component of mental health. "Being yourself" involves having your own natural thoughts, feelings, perceptions, needs, wants, and motives; acting on these in your own ways in your quest to fulfill your own goals; and developing your potentials in the directions that you choose. Being yourself is a rewarding and joyful experience because it involves being able to fully appreciate all of who you are and what you do for yourself.

"Not being yourself" involves denying or avoiding some or all of your own thoughts, feelings, perceptions, needs, wants, and motives, and acting as others want you to act instead of in ways that would express the real you and be in your best interest. "Not being yourself" leads to feelings of fear of showing your true self, guilt over betraying yourself and for not being "good enough" for others, shame for denying yourself, feeling like an imposter, anger and hatred toward yourself as well as those who do not accept your real self, and lowered self-esteem. As an example, if you believe that in order to maintain parental acceptance you must go to college instead of pursuing the carpentry that feels right for you, and you go against your natural choice, then you will hate yourself and your parents for it. Not being yourself also restricts your chances to build good self-esteem, because you associate the positive consequences of your actions when not being yourself with the false self that you have presented to the world, rather than with the real self that is your fundamental identity.

Since we know that in growing up we must adapt to what parents and society want from us, which is often different from what we would naturally do, how can we possibly be our natural selves? Fortunately, we have so many potentials that much of what others want from us are behaviors and perceptions that are adequately natural to us, produce some rewards for us as well as for others, and do not present us with significant conflict. For example, we can learn any language, so the requirement that we use the language of those around us is not a conflict for us. Fortunately, most children are able to accommodate to reasonable parental and societal requirements and still be themselves enough that they can feel a significant amount of pleasure about being themselves. No one is truly himself all the time, because such a person could not exist in society with others. Neither extreme is healthy. If you give up self entirely, then you will not develop adequately as a separate person, and if you fight against making any accommodations to what others require, then you will have intense emotional problems concerning acceptance-rejection issues. For most children the solution is to accommodate as necessary outwardly, while maintaining a jealously guarded and partly hidden real self, which the child hopes can be expressed more fully when he or she has more independence as an adult.

For example, if we are pressured to "love" Aunt Martha, when Aunt Martha is truly a nasty woman who hurts others' feelings constantly, if we go along with what is wanted by our family, we may hate ourselves for doing so. Most people solve this problem by pretending to "love"

Aunt Martha-as long as that does not take up more than a few minutes each year-and will in their hearts continue to be clear with themselves that Aunt Martha is a destructive and thoroughly disagreeable woman.

Being yourself requires that you make your own decisions, rather than just doing what others want, and this is sometimes difficult, such as having to choose for yourself what is the right thing to do or what is the best thing to do for yourself, especially when doing what you would like to do could lead to harm to someone else or to conflict with others. If you practice, though, you can learn to make good decisions.

In each circumstance you face, decide whether to conform to others' wishes or go your own way on the basis of what is in your overall best interest. Balance the gain from doing what others want against the loss of self that will be involved. In many instances we gain more by doing what others want, and in many instances we can do what others want without feeling like we are betraying ourselves. If the cost of going against our real selves is too great, though, we must honor who we really are.

In conforming to what our parents and society want, we can lose track of our real selves. If we pay attention, however, we can tell whether we are being adequately true to ourselves, because actions that are not consonant with our real selves result in such things as a feeling of disgust or distaste for what we are doing, self-dislike, inner conflict and upset, guilt over self-betrayal, and outcomes that are not good for us. We know deep down when an action violates our standards or what we believe in, when it does not represent how we want to view ourselves, or when it is not in our long-term best interest.

Reclaiming Your Right to Be Yourself

If you suffer from not being yourself, you can reclaim your right to be yourself, by reversing the direction of the obligation you have felt to do what others want, acting on your real perceptions, feelings, thoughts, needs/wants, and motives, and developing your real potentials. "Reversing the obligation" means that instead of believing that you must act like others want you to act so they won't reject you, you will now act in ways that are true to yourself, while expecting them to accept the real you. Instead of you feeling obligated to deny your true self so that they will be happy, you now assume that they are obligated to accept you as you are, so that you can be emotionally healthy!

Sometimes others claim that we are harming them when we do what is right for us, such as when your mother claims that you are "killing" her by moving out of her home at 27 to have your own life. You are not intending to hurt her—you simply want to live your own life. In this circumstance, you must use your independent mind to decide whose right takes precedence. Since most people in our society accept the right of everyone to eventually move out of their parents' homes and have their own lives, your right to be yourself is more important than and takes precedence over your mother's right not to feel emotional pain. In general we expect people to be primarily responsible themselves for their own feelings and emotional well-being.

If your family views this differently, it will be a special challenge for you to change your thinking about this and to work out how to be yourself in your family, but you do deserve the right to be yourself.

Finding Out Who You Are and Developing the Real You

If you feel restricted from being your real self, then be more of who you want to be, since this will express important core aspects of yourself that have been hidden and rejected up to now. Take a good look at yourself and decide whether you are being yourself in a healthy way, or whether you are mostly trying to be what others want you to be. You can ask these questions. Do you like yourself as you are? Do you enjoy being yourself? Who do you really want to be now? Are there ways that you present yourself to others that you know are fake (like pretending to like your friends when in fact you think they are shallow, boring, and untrustworthy)? Do you respect yourself as you are?

Identify parts of yourself that have been rejected or undeveloped. Consider characteristics that you reject because your parents did not like them, and consider whether those characteristics could express aspects of your real self. Think about choices that you have made basically because others wanted you to, and consider who you might have become if you had gone the other way. You can look for these parts in activities, hobbies, and careers that truly interest you; emotions, values, beliefs, and passions that appeal to you; personal qualities that you admire; and types of relationships that interest you. Perhaps you stopped expressing affection because your family ridiculed men who showed emotion, or perhaps you became passive instead of assertive because your mother was weak and was afraid of anyone who was assertive. You have the right to consider whether you now wish to express your affection more openly, and whether you wish to be more assertive. Perhaps you would like to learn about classical music, or learn to play the guitar, or go camping, or learn to crochet, or be a "big brother" to a young boy. Whatever would feel good to you as an expression of the real you is what you should try out (assuming, of course, that it does not directly harm someone else). Don't restrict your thinking in any way when you seek awareness of your neglected potentials.

Notice when and how you keep yourself from expressing the real you. Stop any criticizing or rejecting of yourself that you do when you try out new expressions of the real you. As long as you are not inappropriately harming anyone else by being yourself, you have a right to do it, regardless of whether others like it. Practice supporting, comforting, and loving yourself in place of punishing yourself for being the real you.

Devote some time to being and expressing those important aspects of yourself that you want to develop. Join a bicycle club, learn to paint, tell each of your friends why they are important to you—anything that you want to develop as a part of yourself. Find out more about who you really are, and enjoy being the real you! Your self-esteem will benefit.

Deal with your fear that you will displease others if you are your real self. You must believe that you will get more from the joy of being yourself than you will from continuing to restrict yourself in order to earn conditional acceptance from those who do not like who you really are. Don't allow others' negative reactions to deter you. They will have to either adjust or stop being around you so much. Your right to be yourself takes precedence over their desire to be more comfortable by having you continue to not be yourself. You will feel good about standing up for the real you!

Develop the sensitivity to recognize instantly when others are trying to get you to be what they want you to be, the self-knowledge to know quickly whether it will be good for the real you to go along with these pressures (sometimes it is, and sometimes it isn't good for you to do what others want), and the strength to say "no" when going along with what others want will not be good for you. If you are in the habit of doing or being whatever others want, begin to notice when you do this, and think later about whether it is what you really want to do. If you don't want to do these behaviors, then next time tell others that "It is not good for me" to do these things, or "It doesn't feel right for me" to do them, or "I don't like myself when I do this, so I'm not going to do it."

Allow others the same right to be themselves as you have to be yourself. If it's OK for you to be yourself, then it's OK for others to be themselves, too. This may require you to become more comfortable with a wider range of behaviors or feelings. You are not required, however, to be around people you don't like or who have a negative influence on you, if you don't want to.

Your Rights

You have the right to exist, the right to define yourself as you wish to be defined (instead of accepting others' views of you as the truth about you), the right to be yourself (as long as this does not clearly and directly harm someone else), the right to equal treatment, the right to all of the good things in life that are available to everyone, and the right to the conditions of basic respect, acceptance, and equality that build good self-esteem. If you have been deprived of these rights, or if you have failed to claim these rights, then it is time to claim them now. Your self-esteem will grow from it!

Step 6

Respect Yourself

All must respect those who respect themselves.
—Christian Nestal Bovee

Do you respect yourself? Do you treat yourself with respect? Or, do you typically feel the opposite of self-respect—shame and inferiority? The dictionary defines "respect" (in the sense that we are concerned with) as holding someone in esteem or in high regard. "To esteem" means to set a high value on and to regard highly and prize accordingly. When you respect someone, then, you hold him in high or special regard, set a high value on him, and regard him as valuable.

To respect yourself, then, is to hold yourself in high or special regard, set a high value on yourself, and regard yourself as valuable. It is undoubtedly true that you are very valuable to yourself, since you have the greatest potential of anyone in the world to produce good outcomes for yourself. Just think of the many things you already do that are beneficial for yourself (even if you do not react to these things with good feelings about yourself now). You find food and shelter for yourself, keep yourself from the worst of harm, and seek at least some minimal level of pleasure for yourself in life. This is all very valuable to you—give yourself credit for it! You are valuable to yourself regardless of whether certain others value you in the way you want them to.

Respect does not imply deference. Some parents punish children into "respecting" them as parents. When these parents say "you should respect me," they actually mean "you should give in to my wishes at all times and never doubt me." This is submission and deference, and not respect at all.

Another common but misleading use of "respect" is to speak of "really respecting" someone when we actually mean that we admire the person—often someone we believe to be very successful in life, like an athlete or entertainment figure. We imagine that their lives are perfect, and we prefer this fantasy to our own normal lives of partial success and partial failure. We think that we could feel good if only our lives were like those of the "rich and famous," but in reality all lives are fundamentally like our lives, and by doing a good job with our lives, we deserve respect and admiration just as much as anyone else.

Learn to Respect Yourself by Treating Yourself with Respect

You can learn the elements of respecting yourself by treating yourself with respect (even if that is hard to do at first), gradually coming to feel respect in response to yourself more and more of the time. To respect yourself is to hold yourself in high regard, set a high value on yourself, and regard yourself as valuable. To get started, it may help to "image your goal" by getting in touch with the feeling of respect as you think of someone you respect. Then, while still feeling those feelings, put yourself in the place of the other person in your mind and practice feeling these feelings regarding yourself. Let yourself experience having these feelings about yourself for a minute. Consider why you don't do this more often. It may be helpful to look in a mirror at yourself while you feel these feelings for yourself. As you look at yourself in the mirror, be aware of all of the good things you do for yourself, and of the untold millions of nice things that you will do for yourself in the future. Feel your value to yourself. You are the most valuable person in the world to yourself. Value yourself.

When you value yourself, you will naturally hold yourself in high regard—seeing yourself as important, special, and worthwhile. You are special and unique. There is no one else just like you, and you can do wonderful things, both for yourself and for others. You are interesting, fascinating, and very valuable to all who benefit from your values and your actions. View yourself in this way—as special, wonderful, and unique, and then feel the warm, positive feelings that follow naturally toward anyone like that.

You would naturally treat someone well whom you valued. You would respect his rights and try not to infringe on the person or cause him distress or discomfort. You would try to make it pleasant for the person and would try to make him comfortable, by treating that person with courtesy and consideration and paying attention to his feelings and needs. Applying this to yourself, treat yourself well. Respect your rights, and don't cause yourself distress or discomfort. Try to make things pleasant and comfortable for yourself. Pay close attention to your feelings and needs, and act to take good care of yourself. Be considerate of yourself, and treat yourself with the same courtesy you give others.

Even though you are a special and valuable person, I am not suggesting that you are any more special, wonderful, valuable, or worthy of respect than anyone else. We all have this fundamental kind of value. You are not wonderful because your mother thinks so, or because you are "better than" your brother. You are special and wonderful just for being you and because you are important to yourself!

What keeps you from respecting yourself-unfamiliarity with feeling self-respect, thinking that it would contradict what certain others feel about you, or thinking that it is too radically different from how you feel about yourself now? Whatever the reason, you have the power to change it. The barriers are within you, and not outside. Respecting yourself takes place totally within you-it is not placed in you or done to you from outside.

If you're afraid to change, it's time to take some risks. If you're afraid to challenge others' disrespectful treatment of you, then perhaps it's time to make a commitment to treat yourself well, rather than to keep others comfortable. If you lived with rattlesnakes, you wouldn't automatically think that it was your obligation to let them bite you! If certain others are disrespecting you, it may be time to demand a change or put some distance between you and them. No one can make you ready to change, of course—it has to be your decision and your commitment, but you will feel so much better respecting yourself than not respecting yourself that I strongly urge you to go for it!

If you are to respect yourself (to regard yourself highly and as being valuable), it is naturally important not to create reasons for devaluing yourself. It is hard to respect yourself if you are behaving in ways that are dishonorable or that arouse feelings of self-contempt or self-dislike. If you are to respect yourself, therefore, it is important to keep a clear conscience—to have reasonable and humane standards, to know clearly what these standards are, and to live up to them.

Treating Everyone with Respect

Knowing how good it feels to respect yourself and to treat yourself with respect, you can give this gift to others by treating everyone with basic respect at all times. This does not require that you personally place a high value on every individual, but simply that you treat them as if they had a high value. You can treat them with courtesy and consideration, honor their rights, and try to make being around you pleasant for them. You can treat them as if they were worthwhile, special, and important. You can pay attention to their feelings and needs and do what you can in small ways to make them comfortable. (Wouldn't it be wonderful if everyone treated everyone else with this basic concern and respect? Fundamental to this book are the beliefs that everyone is of equal value, everyone deserves good self-esteem, and everyone deserves to be treated with respect.)

The social benefits of treating people with respect are tremendous. When people are treated with respect, they tend to treat others with respect, too, and social interactions are much smoother and more productive. When people are not treated with respect, they become upset, fearful, angry, and defensive, and they have many more conflicts. You can improve your relationships with others just by treating others with respect at all times.

Treat everyone with the same basic respect at all times. If you wish to show the higher value you place on some people, use other rewards to show that, while giving everyone the same basic respect.

People often use shaming and disrespect to try to control the behavior of others. Start noticing how people, including yourself, use contempt and purposive disrespect as a way of trying to force others to behave as you want them to. Disrespecting people on purpose is more destructive than it is useful, since it attacks their precious self-esteem and since there are other adequately effective methods of influencing their behavior, such as staying away from people we do not respect or not giving people what they want. It is therefore better for society if we treat everyone—including the criminal and those we hate—with basic respect at all times, even while we administer other punishments or consequences to them.

If others disrespect you, stay clear within yourself that it does not diminish your fundamental value—it only means that others do not at the moment recognize that value. Treat yourself with respect, maintain your dignity, and act as if you deserved respect, regardless of how others are treating you (which will tend to induce others to treat you that way, too).

Respect is fundamental to good self-esteem and good social order.

Work on valuing yourself, holding yourself in high regard, and treating yourself in every other way with respect, at the same time that you contribute to others' self-esteem by treating them with respect, too. You will feel better, and you will be making a better world!

Step 7

Accept Yourself (and Forgive Yourself)

There comes a time in each life like a point of fulcrum. At that time you must accept yourself. It is not any more what you will become. It is what you are and always will be.

—John Fowles

Of all the attitudes and feelings about yourself, respecting yourself, accepting yourself, and loving yourself are the three things that are most beneficial for your self-esteem, and among these three, accepting yourself is the most effective.

Being accepted is basically "being allowed"—being allowed to be yourself without rejection or attack. Self-acceptance is therefore "allowing yourself to be" instead of rejecting and attacking yourself. Unfortunately most people attack and reject themselves with alarming frequency. Every time you harm yourself, criticize yourself, put yourself down, or compare yourself unfavorably to someone else, you are rejecting yourself. Every time you feel bad that you are not as good at something as someone else or say to yourself "Boy, that was stupid" (regarding something you have done), "You're really messing up today," "My hair sure looks bad today," or "You're never going to be good enough in this job," you are rejecting yourself. Since as adults we often give ourselves more rejection than others give us, it is even more important to learn to accept ourselves than it is to find acceptance from others!

To achieve acceptance, know yourself completely and intimately (so that you don't pretend that certain things that you dislike about yourself don't even exist); don't react to any parts of yourself that you dislike with attack and rejection; and calmly decide either to work toward changing the disliked or harmful parts of yourself or to simply let them be (which is perfectly OK to do). Stop criticizing yourself and hurting your own feelings. Stop rejecting yourself. The peace and calm of accepting yourself is wonderful.

As an example, Robert felt inferior because he is short, always wondering if other people were noticing his height (even when they usually were not), but Robert learned to accept his relatively short physical stature, so that he doesn't think about it any more and doesn't attack himself for it or feel inferior because of it. He is free to be happily himself just as he is. He still would have preferred to be taller, but he doesn't waste time wishing he had been taller. He doesn't put himself down because of it, and he doesn't feel bad if others notice his height. He accepts himself.

If you are not accepting yourself (letting yourself be), it means that you are rejecting yourself instead. The key to accepting yourself, then, is to stop rejecting yourself. Think seriously about this, and try to identify the ways in which you reject yourself. The most common types of self-rejecting behaviors are self-criticism, self-accusations, harming oneself, punishing oneself, and demeaning oneself by calling oneself names or putting oneself in negative or inferior positions. How do you do these things to yourself? What do you criticize yourself for?

The primary reason that we reject ourselves is that we have learned from those around us to reject and criticize ourselves, either because we believe that we do not meet expected standards, that we have done something wrong, or that it is simply "wrong" to be ourselves. Some people also reject themselves because they believe that constantly rejecting themselves is the only way to control their "bad" behavior. These reasons for rejecting ourselves are false and unnecessary.

Self-critical and self-rejecting behaviors are learned from those around us, usually in childhood. If significant others view us and treat us as if we deserve criticism and demeanment, for our behavior or simply for being ourselves, then as we grow up we begin to criticize and demean ourselves. Every time we "make a mistake" (every time we notice the displeased or disapproving reactions of others) we may tell ourselves something unrealistic and excessive, like "Boy, am I stupid," "I'll never get it right," "I'm terrible," or some other self-demeaning statement. The key to change is recognizing that you do not deserve this self-criticism and demeanment—that your behavior is not "bad" or at least not bad enough to justify rejecting yourself, and that you are actually an OK person.

Acceptance is often confused with approval and other positive responses from others. Being approved of involves being measured against the standards of others and being preferred or rejected by them, while acceptance is "being allowed to be" just as you are. Being accepted does not imply that everything about you is OK with others. You can be accepted without being approved of by others.

You probably believe that if you don't get the approval, or at least the acceptance, of certain important others, then you are worthless and should feel inferior and undeserving, but this is totally false. Your value and your happiness do not depend on the approval or acceptance of specific other people. Since you are no longer a child, your survival and gratifications no longer depend primarily on certain other individuals, like your parents. You can do very well without any of those people who reject you, if you are only willing to do so. Use your independent mind to realize that you are OK even without these other people. Give up worrying about gaining their approval and acceptance (which you actually already deserve), and focus on your own acceptance of yourself and on making your life a good life to live. Mourn for what you have not had, and mourn for the hope that you are now giving up of getting it from those people, and then rejoice in your new freedom to be yourself and to do what is good for you!

To change your mind about yourself—to see yourself as basically OK rather than as a terrible person or a screw-up—requires questioning the standards and the attitudes of those who first rejected and criticized you. You must be able to see that there was in fact nothing much wrong with you, even though certain adults may have had negative feelings and attitudes toward you, which were their own responsibility and were not really due to anything significant about you. By itself, the fact that you were rejected proves nothing about you. Realistically search your memory and your assumptions about yourself, and you will not find much really wrong with you. (In those few cases in which a part of yourself could lead to harm to others— e.g., a sexual interest exclusively in children, it will serve you best to accept that part of yourself within yourself, while at the same time ensuring that no one is harmed by it.)

People over-generalize a great deal about their lack of worth, with such false statements as:

"I'm terrible"

"I'm worthless", and

"I'm not acceptable."

You must question and correct your over-generalizations. You may not have been accepted by your mother, your father, or certain other important people, but that does not mean that you are "not acceptable" in general. *You are acceptable just the way you are, even if your parents did not accept you.*

Imagine what it would feel like to cease criticizing yourself and finding fault with yourself. The peace would be wonderful! You could relax instead of always being on guard or always having to answer your own criticisms and doubts. You could really live your life, instead of being perpetually distracted by your own internal criticisms. Give it a try. You are OK. There is nothing really wrong with you. Work on stopping your unnecessary self-criticism and self-demeanment. "Let yourself be" (allow yourself to be), without self-criticism and self-demeanment. You will love yourself for it!

Some people justify rejecting themselves (and justify others' rejection of them) on the basis that they are not "good enough" and therefore deserve to be criticized and rejected, but this idea is simply based on using inappropriate standards. If appropriate standards are used, you are good enough. Changing this requires questioning and changing the standards that you apply to yourself. (See Step 9 for a complete discussion of appropriate and inappropriate standards.) Some people hold onto patterns of self-rejection because they think that it is easier to reject themselves than it would be to fully recognize how they are being rejected by their parents or others they love. They make their rejection of themselves their own fault, and as long as they continue to try to force themselves to be who they are "supposed to be," they don't have to recognize and deal with the pain of the actual rejection that they are getting. If we stop rejecting ourselves, we will see more clearly the inappropriateness of how we are being rejected by others, and we will probably feel some sadness and anger about it.

People who have been rejected sometimes feel that they do not deserve to be members of their families or of society. If you treat others decently, you do deserve to be accepted (allowed to be) as a member of your family and of society, regardless of the attitudes and reactions of anyone else to the contrary. You are as good as anyone else deep down, and you deserve equal treatment just as much as anyone else. Assert your right to be an equal member, and behave as a good group member should.

Controlling Yourself Through Self-Criticism and Self-Rejection

As children we all must learn to conform to adult social expectations, and one of the methods some people use to control their unacceptable behavior is constantly watching themselves for things to reject themselves for. You think that if you constantly look for faults or something wrong with yourself, then you can "catch yourself" before you do anything wrong, and you won't have much opportunity to engage in any really "bad" behavior. Unfortunately your suspicious habits of self-criticism and self-punishment will also cause you to be unable to accept yourself!

It is unnecessary to use self-rejection as a means of controlling your behavior, because as an adult you can choose your appropriate behaviors on the basis of what is in your best interest. In fact, you should always do what is in your best interest! (Some will disagree with this last statement, but I invite them to consider a change in perspective. We always do what we perceive to be in our best interest—it's just that we don't always identify it that way (so that we won't seem "selfish"). This new method of controlling yourself will be explained in Step 10.)

Some people fear that if they accept themselves, they will accept their bad behavior as well (and will therefore do more bad behavior). This is not a problem of acceptance but of knowing what is best for you. If you believe deep down that your bad behavior is best for you, then you will continue to do it. Your conflict is between what you believe you should do and what you really believe is best for you. You will be more comfortable with yourself if you resolve this inner conflict. If your bad behavior is actually bad for you, you must recognize this and decide whether you are going to what is best for you or what is bad for you. If your bad behavior is actually good for you, then there is something wrong with the rules you are trying to live by!

Some people fear that if they accept themselves they will become lazy and complacent and will never make any further improvements in themselves. Actually, meaningful change is easier in an accepting climate than it is in a rejecting climate. A rejecting, punishing climate motivates us to escape the punishment, but the anger and resentment that we feel about the rejection and punishment also cause us to stiffen up and refuse to change (since "giving in" to the pressure to change would be like completely giving up control and giving up self-respect). In an accepting climate, we do not have to fight back, we are free to consider who we really want to be and what would be best for us, and we are free to make those changes if we wish.

Forgiving Yourself

It is typical for us to feel guilt or shame when we do something in conflict with our standards, harm ourselves or others, or reject ourselves. Guilt (a combination of fear, anticipation of punishment, and painful self-criticism) is a primary barrier to self-acceptance, and in order to restore inner peace and accept ourselves fully once again, it is important to forgive ourselves. Here are some steps that will help you in seeking forgiveness—from yourself or from others—so that you can accept yourself once again.

In dealing with guilt,

(1) acknowledge fully and honestly what you have done, with no excuses, rationalizations, or attempts to shift the blame inappropriately to others. (Of course, you should not take responsibility for things that you have <u>not</u> done!)

(2) Determine how your behavior has affected both yourself and others. If no one has been harmed, then reconsider whether what you have done is actually "wrong." If others act hurt, but this is because of their own inappropriate reactions to your behavior, then you must draw the line regarding what you will be responsible for.

(3) Consciously accept what you did as part of your history now. Don't pretend that it didn't happen, or that it really wasn't you, or that you can wipe out your action by making up for it after the fact.

(4) Understand why you did what you did. What needs, motives, weaknesses, and blind spots were involved? Be totally honest with yourself. This is where you are likely to see how you hurt yourself sometimes with your choices.

(5) Consider whether the standard you applied to yourself was appropriate, and consider whether you have been too hard on yourself.

(6) If you believe that your standard is appropriate, and you still feel uncomfortable with your behavior, then you must next decide whether you want to change your behavior. Carefully decide if it

would really be better for you if you did not do that behavior again. This is a crucial step, for if you really think, consciously or unconsciously, that it is better for you to keep doing the behavior, then you will keep on doing it (and keep on violating the standards that you say you believe in), even if it results in guilt over and over again.

(7) If you decide not to do the behavior again, resolve to take better care of yourself in the future by not repeating the behavior in question, and commit yourself to this path.

(8) Decide whether you need to change some of your habits and ways of controlling your behavior in order to be able to avoid this particular behavior in the future.

(9) Consider taking actions to make up for what you have done, like apologizing or making something up to another person (or to yourself, if you were the one harmed).

(10) You have now done all you can do to take care of what you have done and to avoid doing such things in the future. The last step is to accept the above steps as adequate grounds for letting go of that past behavior, letting go of any guilt that you feel, receiving the forgiveness of the other person if that is offered, and forgiving yourself— which means accepting yourself as OK again.

If you have trouble forgiving yourself, or finding forgiveness from others, identify the conditions that you require in order to be forgiven. Do you have some unrealistic requirements that are not likely to be met, such as requiring that you repay the injured party double value before you can forgive yourself, or requiring that the person injured tell you that you are OK? Also, you may need to accept that sometimes the injured party is spiteful and refuses to forgive. Sometimes forgiving yourself is your only option.

You can forgive yourself for harming yourself accidentally if you sincerely intend not to continue harming yourself, but if you are fooling yourself when you promise yourself not to repeat the self-harming behavior, eventually this will become an issue of bad faith with yourself. You will be unable to fool yourself any longer and unable to accept yourself.

In forgiving ourselves, we see clearly what we have done, we right wrongs that can be righted, we improve our behavior for the future so that we will not harm ourselves or others in the same way again, and then we let go of guilt and self-hatred and move forward into the future with a positive though realistic attitude.

Adjusting to Accepting Yourself

If you fully accept that you were OK and that you have not really deserved to feel bad about yourself all these years, you will feel much sadness, and you may feel anger toward those who convinced you that you were "bad" or inferior. Both of these feelings are normal, and it is best that you let yourself feel them fully and wait for them to pass. This sadness is both a release of a tremendous amount of stored up pain and a readjustment to a new identity. For years you have been whipping yourself to be someone else, because you thought that you were not good enough or were not who you were supposed to be. Now you are accepting that you will never be good enough according to those previous, inappropriate requirements and that you will never please those whom you have been striving to please. Naturally you will feel sadness at giving this up, but you will also feel release and relaxation at letting go of the pressure of these impossible expectations and accepting that you are OK just the way you are. As to the anger, just because you feel anger does not mean that you must act on it. If you do feel impelled to act, it will be enough to tell those who have not accepted you that in your opinion they were wrong about you and that they harmed you greatly. Let yourself feel these feelings, take action if you need to, and wait for the feelings to pass, for they will pass.

Summary and Startling Conclusion

The following fact is so amazing that it must be stated over and over-all you need to do in order to accept yourself is to stop rejecting yourself and allow yourself to be. Stop criticizing and demeaning yourself. Accept the fact that it is OK not to be totally OK even if certain other people are not happy with you. It is not true that you are unacceptable because there is "something wrong with you." There is nothing wrong with you. You have taken on the irrational and idiosyncratic negative responses of certain others to you, and you have been rejecting yourself for no reason. There is nothing so wrong with you that you deserve this rejection. Lighten up. Work on seeing yourself more realistically—not through the eyes of those rejecting adults of your childhood, but through your more realistic and understanding eyes. Let yourself be (while still refraining from harming others). Take the risk of accepting an imperfect but perfectly OK human being—yourself. (Remember, though, if you are harming yourself through your choices and behaviors, you will very naturally be unable to accept yourself.)

In place of criticizing yourself, give yourself support and love. In place of demeaning yourself, appreciate your many good qualities and learn to do a good job at deciding and doing what is best for you. In place of punishing yourself, have compassion for yourself and forgive and comfort yourself. Treat yourself with the same caring, consideration, and thoughtfulness that you would another person whom you love. Redefine yourself as OK and worthy of inclusion with others. Forgive yourself for the pain you have caused yourself by rejecting yourself. Give yourself the gift of believing that it is really OK to be who you are! Allow yourself to be!

All you have to do in order to accept yourself is to stop rejecting yourself and let yourself be!

Step 8

Love Yourself

Above all things, reverence yourself.

—Pythagoras

Feeling loved is perhaps the most wonderful and treasured of feelings. Love truly "makes the world go round," and it provides most of us with our clearest reason for experiencing life as worthwhile. Since love is so important, it is crucial for good mental health and good self-esteem that we learn to love ourselves—particularly so that we can count on our love for ourselves when we are not receiving love from others. And, you will find that loving yourself is an excellent way to attract others to loving relationships with you.

For our purposes love will be defined as a positive, warm, affectionate feeling involving attachment feelings, identification with the loved one, desire to be close or closer with the loved one, the wish for good things for the loved one, and pleasure experienced in contact with or contemplation of the loved one. Love is a warm, positive feeling. When we love someone we feel warmly toward him or her, and it feels good. Similarly when we love ourselves, we feel warm toward ourselves, and it feels good. We feel affection (tender attachment and fondness) for ourselves.

When we love, we want to attach to the loved one and to be connected. When we love ourselves, we want to be firmly connected with ourselves, rather than keeping ourselves at arm's length because we see ourselves as unworthy and undesirable. We know that we are wonderful and lovable, despite our flaws and occasional failures, and we are glad to attach to ourselves and to give ourselves the support and affirmation that attachment involves.

When we love, we want to be like the loved one or identified with the loved one, since it feels good to be connected in this way, and since it feels good to think of ourselves as similar to the loved one. In loving ourselves, we identify clearly with ourselves, knowing who we are, accepting all parts of ourselves, and valuing and affirming who we are by identifying with ourselves.

In loving, we want to be close to the loved one. Being near feels good and is comforting. In loving ourselves, we revel in being close with ourselves. Since we enjoy ourselves and find ourselves valuable, it is enjoyable to be close with ourselves—to enjoy all the little things we do or notice about ourselves, to appreciate our abilities and the things we do for ourselves, and to grow ever closer and more acquainted with ourselves because we are interesting, valuable, and wonderful.

When we love someone, we want good things for him or her. We want the person to be happy and fortunate in life, and we want things to go well for him or her. We feel pain empathically when a loved person is hurt. Similarly when we love ourselves, we want good things for ourselves. We know that we deserve all the good in life that is available, and our wishes for ourselves are unequivocally positive. We feel compassion and pain for ourselves when we are hurt.

We take great pleasure in our contact with the loved one, and we often enjoy simply looking at or thinking about the loved person, even when not interacting. The loved person is a positive object for us whom we value as a source of good feelings and pleasant experiences. When we love ourselves, we enjoy being in contact with ourselves. We enjoy being aware of ourselves, observing our actions and being aware of every feeling and thought inside. We are interesting to ourselves, and because we are positive objects for ourselves, being aware of ourselves is pleasurable. (Pleasure in awareness of self may arouse prejudices about narcissism (being overly self-involved) for some, but if we are positive objects for ourselves, then it logically follows that being aware of ourselves will be a positive experience, which is our fundamental definition of self-esteem.)

Ideally, our love for ourselves and for specific others can generalize to become a loving attitude toward everyone and toward life itself. You probably know certain people who seem to have this generally loving attitude, and they make the world a better place. This general attitude of love is rooted in love for oneself.

The concept of love used here emphasizes the affectionate and giving aspects of love. This affectionate love feels wonderful and is not a mixed positive and negative experience. That which is negative or painful is not love. The pain of unrequited love, for example, is not pain resulting from love but is rather the pain of not getting what we want. In loving yourself, having that love returned will not be a problem!

For some of us, love becomes associated with sexual arousal or with negative feelings such as pain, shame, or fear, if these other feelings are regularly present in our early years when we feel loved. We must learn to be clear that love is not these other feelings, and that we do not have to continue to feel these other feelings when we feel love. Even if negative feelings associated with love frighten you when you seek love from others, your love for yourself can be safe and dependable.

Love in our culture is often seen as including physical desire or sexual passion as well as affectionate love, but these are quite different in a very important way. We know that passion is inconstant and that the affectionate aspects of love can be more enduring. The most important distinction between passion/desire and affectionate love, though, is that desire and passion want something _from_the loved one, while affectionate love wants something _for_ the loved one. Loving someone and wanting someone to love us are two different things.

Love as affection does not require that the loved one be a certain way or give something back. Don't try to love yourself for being the person someone else wants you to be if that is not your true self. You are lovable just as you are, and you don't have to change in order to love yourself!

Loving oneself is sometimes called selfish by others, but people who call you selfish for loving yourself are usually trying to make you dependent on them and their "love" (or approval) which they will give you only if you do what they want. Love for a price is not worth much.

Loving oneself is sometimes called self-centered, but since people who love themselves are more loved than those who are dependent totally on others for love, people who love themselves should therefore be better able to love, pay attention to, and give to others!

You do not have to be perfect to love yourself. Just as you can love others and know their imperfections at the same time, you can love yourself just as you are and still know that there are things about yourself that you dislike or wish to change.

You don't have to prove anything or meet any standard in order to love yourself. You don't have to get good grades or be successful or please your mother in order to love yourself. True love is not given for meeting standards. You are lovable all the time—not just when you meet standards. (It will, of course, be hard to love yourself if you perceive yourself as doing things that harm yourself.)

You don't have to do anything to deserve love, and if you have not been loved it does not mean that there is something wrong with you. We have addressed in earlier chapters the false belief that there was something wrong with you that caused and causes you not to be worthy of love and other good things in life. Every child deserves love and nurturance.

You deserved love as a child, and you are deserving of love now just the way you are. There is nothing "wrong" with you that "makes" people reject and not love you.

Barriers to Loving Yourself

For most of us, self-rejection (not accepting ourselves) is the primary barrier to loving ourselves and to accepting love from others. If you reject yourself and do not accept yourself, then it seems inappropriate to be loved. You think, "I'm bad" [or "I'm not good enough," or "I'm worthless," etc.], so I should hate myself and reject myself. Since I'm so bad, no one could or should love me, and I could not possibly love myself." As discussed previously, these explanations of why we are not lovable are false, but having some reason for why we do not deserve love makes it easier to accept our deprivation and easier not to oppose the rejecting attitudes of others. If we believe that it is our own fault that we are not loved or accepted, then we think we should blame ourselves and not blame those who actually created the problem! In addition, we would rather have an explanation for why we were not loved, even if it is incorrect, than not to "know" why! Having an explanation also means that we are in control of what we need to do in order to be loved. We think that if we could only change our "bad" features (be nicer, look prettier, follow the rules better, get better grades, etc.), then we would be loved and accepted. Of course, we will not be loved for making these changes, but we can deceive ourselves about being in control by continuing to believe that it is our fault. Affectionate love is not earned!

It is crucial to accept yourself in order to love yourself and accept love from others. As explained in the previous chapter, accepting yourself requires only that you stop rejecting yourself and let yourself be, without attack or criticism. You must come to see that the "reasons" that you think justify rejecting yourself are not sufficient reasons at all—that you are OK just the way you are. Every child is lovable and deserves love.

For some people the pain of past rejections and hurt creates a fear of loving and being loved. One's own love for oneself has clear advantages in this regard. You should be able to depend on your love more than you can on anyone else's. Once you believe that you deserve love just as you are, and you accept your own love as valuable, you need not worry about whether any particular others will love you at any particular time, because you can always love yourself.

If you wish to become able to let others love you again, you must let yourself experience the old pain so that it can pass. You think that you can't stand the pain, but you can. If you let yourself experience the pain, it will run its course and decline, like a river that temporarily floods but goes back to its previous size, and you will find a new way to understand what happened to you in the past. The pain is not going to drive you crazy or make you do things you don't want to do, and it is not going to kill you. Like all other emotional pain, it must be accepted and borne until it goes away and until we learn new ways of handling it. (Dr. Ed Edelhofer has done some inspiring work in helping people with this fear and avoidance.) If you need someone else's support while you let yourself experience this pain, find a friend or counselor to help you.

You may feel that you can't feel loved because you haven't felt loved by anyone and you have never known anyone else to love you. If you are interested in feeling love, though, you already have some yearning or imagination deep down of what love might feel like, because without some sort of image of love, you would not even be interested in being loved. In addition, you have observed others whom you thought were feeling loved, and you have observed those who were loving them, so you have empathic ideas and feelings about what it is like to feel loved and what it is like to love. Seriously explore these ideas and feelings, to clarify what you want.

Another major barrier that we set up to being loved and to loving ourselves is insisting that we will only accept love if it is in a certain form, if it is guaranteed to last forever, or if it comes from a certain person (unless my father loves me, I will remain unlovable, no matter how many other people love me). Clearly these restrictions cut you off from many opportunities for love, including your own love for yourself. To give up these restrictions, you must give up the hope of getting what you have always wanted. You wanted your father's love very much, and you decided that because he didn't love you, you must be worthless, so he is the key to making you worthwhile and lovable. However, you were wrong when you set up this condition. You don't need your father's love in particular-you need simply to feel loved and special. The fact that your father did not love you did not prove anything about you, and his loving you now would not "prove" anything about you, either. Receiving love from yourself is just as worthwhile as receiving it from someone else.

You may hope that getting love in a certain format or from a certain person will right a wrong that has been done to you. You will hold out forever, depriving yourself of love, until you get the love you deserved originally. Your self-deprivation is supposed to induce guilt in your father, so that he will realize his mistake and come around to loving you now. Unfortunately, in real life this rarely succeeds, and you are depriving yourself of love needlessly. You must accept that you can't get now what you should have gotten—that even though it was unfair and was not your fault, you are helpless to change what happened, and it is not going to be made up to you. This is a lot to face, but you must accept it.

When people don't want their own love and insist that love must come from others, it usually means that since they see themselves as worthless, they think that their own love must be worthless, too. Actually, your own love is just as valuable (and a lot more trustworthy) than the love of others, wonderful as that love from others can be sometimes. The nice things that you do for yourself because you love yourself are just as valuable as the nice things that others do for you. We value others' love more highly because we put extra meaning on it, e.g. that being loved by mother means not just that someone loves us, but also that we are special and that life is secure. These extra inferences are usually realistically false (even though these false beliefs can sometimes be helpful in our coping), and you can find specialness and security without them. You are already lovable, you are special, and life is reasonably secure whether or not your mother loved you. Your own love for yourself is always with you and is the most dependable love you can have, and you are special to yourself. Work on loving yourself and enjoying it!

People who have been significantly abused may think later that they can only receive love if they are also being hurt. Those for whom love has been intertwined with self-sacrifice or other forms of manipulation can have a similar problem. We can understand how these people might shy away from love because of their belief that love hurts and hurts greatly.

If love is too closely associated for you with some negative experience or emotion, then your challenge is to look back and re-conceptualize what happened in your life. Using our description of love above, re-think your experience. Identify the love as love, and be willing to identify the abuse, self-sacrifice, etc., as exactly what it was. Separate them in your mind. The same person may have loved you at some moments and wanted to hurt you at others, but this doesn't mean that love and pain must go together. When she loved you, she loved you, and when she hurt you, she hurt you. They are two different things. The harm that others do to you is never OK, and you do not have to accept harm or hurt in order to be loved. Love is never pain.

Those who have been seriously hurt by their parents may be unable to take a loving parent role with respect to themselves, because they feel toward themselves like their actual parents did who hurt them so much. It is essential that you be yourself and not be your parents who hurt you. Find out what you really feel and think about yourself, as differentiated from what your parents felt or did. If you need to imitate someone, imitate parents who do love their children and treat them lovingly. Also, there may be another older person who loved you— an aunt, a grandfather, etc.—whose role you can take in being a loving parent to yourself.

If you need to separate love from hurt, you must be willing to feel the hurt. You may be very afraid to feel your hurt, but you need to accept the hurt as something that truly happened, but for which you were not responsible, so that you can allow yourself to deserve love without the hurt. If you need the support of someone else while you do this, find that person (perhaps a therapist). The pain may be terrible, but it won't kill you.

Sometimes we reject love in the present out of loyalty to significant others who have not loved us adequately in the past. The child may feel so fiercely loyal to her parents that she insists that even though they did not love her, nothing better can possibly be available, because what her parents provided must have been OK. The child refuses to acknowledge the inadequacies of the parents and prefers not to be loved rather than admit that her parents did a poor job (or give up her hope that they really could love her but just haven't gotten around to it yet).

It's OK to see the inadequacies of your parents. It is not an insult to them for you to see them as they really are, and seeing them realistically does not mean that you do not love them. They can take care of themselves, just as we all must ultimately do, and seeing reality more clearly can help you to feel better about yourself.

Learning To Love Yourself

You can learn to love yourself well and to love others well. The first step in this process is to be clear about what affectionate love is—a warm, positive affectionate feeling that involves attachment feelings, identification with the loved one, desire to be close or closer to the loved one, the wish for good things for the loved one, and pleasure experienced in contact with or contemplation of the loved one. Let yourself meditate on your image of the love you want. Slow down, relax yourself (lying down is probably best), and travel downward inside yourself to those images and feelings. They may be somewhat painful, because of the unfulfilled nature of your longing, but you will survive. Let yourself learn from the knowledge deep within you. Imagine how it feels to be loved and how you would want to be loved. See clearly the barriers you have to feeling loved.

In working on warmth and positivity toward yourself, you can use a source that is within you of warmth and warm feelings, for yourself and for the world. It's glow will warm you and those around you. For most people the bodily location of this source is in the chest (heart) or stomach (center of the body) areas. Focus on the warmth you already have in those areas. Work on relaxing and allowing the warmth to build and come closer to the surface. Let yourself connect this warmth with your self and feel affection for yourself, including tenderness, fondness, and compassion for yourself.

Next, examine your concept of love to see if it differs from affectionate love in ways that are keeping you from trying to love yourself or accepting love from others, and to see if you are expecting the impossible or placing unnecessary requirements on love (such as that you meet certain standards before loving yourself or that love be never-ending).

Experiment with feeling love. For most people with poor self-esteem it will be easier to first feel love for someone else, before feeling love for oneself. Focus on feeling love for someone else until you can feel a clear feeling of love.

Then, generate the same feeling of love for yourself. Think of how valuable and worthwhile you are to yourself and how much you want yourself to be happy, and build these positive feelings and wishes into the feeling of love. It may help you to first generate the feeling of love toward someone else, and then switch the focus of your feeling quickly to yourself while you are still experiencing this love.

Try imagining yourself as a parent feeling love for a baby or a young child—warmth and affection and the desire to nurture and to make things good for this child, who is the most wonderful, special thing in the whole world. Then, as soon as this feeling is clear and strong, focus on the feelings of the child and feel the goodness of being loved—the positive, warm glow of pleasure and security and relaxation that comes from feeling loved. Go back and forth several times between these feelings. Enjoy them. (If you are completely unable to generate a feeling of love within yourself, it may be that your barriers or prior conditioning are too strong to overcome on your own. Consult a therapist about what needs to be done.)

Some people with poor self-esteem had parents who felt love for them but could not show or express it emotionally, and some of these children concluded, falsely, that their parents did not love them ("I must be worthless—even my own parents can't love me," etc.). If this happened to you, as an adult you may be able to look back more objectively at what actually happened and change your mind about whether your parents loved you.

Naturally, in trying to feel love for yourself, you will encounter whatever barriers you have about loving yourself—you aren't valuable enough, you aren't lovable, you're too embarrassed to be loved by anyone, people shouldn't love themselves, etc., etc. Recognize these barriers as they come up, and work on them, re-reading relevant parts of this book if needed. As you practice feeling warm, positive, affectionate feelings toward yourself, you will find opportunities to weed out more of your self-criticism and self-rejection. You deserve love, from others and from yourself.

You will find both progress and difficulties as you try to love yourself. The process can be like "two steps forward and one step back." You acknowledge that you want love. You try loving yourself or accepting love from others, and you find that you are blocking yourself or you encounter some old pain that seems insurmountable. You pause to work on your self-blocking or to get through some of the old pain. You examine the barriers and work on them—establishing new thoughts, beliefs, and attitudes that give you enough support and confidence to try loving, even though you may still feel afraid, and then you try loving again. You make some progress, but then you come up against other fears or blocks and more old pain. You repeat the process. This is the only way to clear things up, but it can be discouraging at times. Remember and hold onto the fact that you can get through the barriers to being able to love yourself and others and to being able to accept love gladly from others. You can do it. Give yourself time, and don't give up.

If you cannot love yourself because there are parts of you that you hate or reject, reconsider your attitude. Compassion and love are always preferable to hate and rejection. Embark on an expedition to reclaim all rejected parts of yourself. You suffer in proportion to the amount of yourself that you reject, because you cannot fully accept or love yourself if you identify parts of yourself as unacceptable or unlovable. Your "shameful" parts are lovable as part of the whole you. Even if there are things you want to change about yourself, the "total you" is still acceptable and lovable just the way you are today.

As you practice feeling love for yourself, add the components of affectional love identified in our definition. First, attach to yourself unconditionally, with no exceptions. Accept all of yourself and view yourself as being valuable and worthwhile, because when you do, you will naturally want to attach and hold on!

Identify with yourself, by recognizing and acknowledging all of yourself, until you can honestly say that you have included all of the various parts of yourself in your self-concept. You must look any parts of yourself that you have rejected squarely in the face and welcome them back, even if you don't like them. You can joyfully claim all of you as being you—not hiding or holding back parts of you from the world but joyfully involving all of yourself in the process of living completely.

Get close to yourself and enjoy it. You are delightful and wonderful, in all of the things you can do and in your own unique and creative ways of perceiving and doing things. Embrace being who you are, and honor all the parts of yourself.

Wish good things for yourself. Obviously if you love yourself, you will want yourself to feel good and to have good things in life. You should be your own best friend and lover, supporter and advocate. You of all people should know what is best for yourself and should proceed to try to get that for yourself.

Take pleasure in contact with and contemplation of yourself. Enjoy simply being aware of yourself. Since you see yourself as wonderful and amazing, you will enjoy being aware of everything you do—feeling your feelings, carrying out actions to benefit yourself and others, thinking, solving problems, etc. Being good company for yourself (since you love, accept, and appreciate yourself), you would naturally enjoy being in contact with yourself. In addition, if you love yourself, then you accept yourself and treat yourself well, and you would naturally then feel pleasure in being in contact with yourself as a person who accepts and loves you and treats you well!

Homework: Do something nice for yourself every day. This may sound simple, but if you have hated yourself or had poor self-esteem, it will not be easy to do. This nice thing you do for yourself each day can be anything you like or enjoy. You might fix something you like for supper, or treat yourself to lunch someplace a little special. You might rent a video movie that you would enjoy. You might spend the evening reading, or go to the gym, or go to a meeting, or go for a walk. The list is almost endless—the only requirement is that you enjoy it, and that you appreciate yourself for giving it to you.

Notice if you put off doing these nice things for yourself with various excuses. You might have been shamed or beaten when you were nice to yourself in the past, so that now you avoid doing nice things for yourself, even though no one would shame you or beat you now (except yourself, of course). We are so good at keeping these feelings buried that we often don't consciously know why we avoid doing nice things for ourselves, but you can usually find out what you are avoiding by going ahead and doing the avoided behavior, because then you will force yourself to feel the feelings you were avoiding, and you will know what you need to overcome.

When you do nice things for yourself, you may find that it's hard to let yourself enjoy the results. Keep thinking to yourself that you do deserve the pleasure, because you do. Try to feel the pleasure, and also allow yourself to feel the sadness, if doing nice things for yourself brings up sad feelings (sadness for all the times you wanted nice things and good feelings for yourself but didn't get them). Most importantly, let yourself feel loved and cared for. You are doing nice things for yourself because you love yourself. As you get more comfortable with doing nice things for yourself, you will naturally do this more and more often, since it makes you feel good.

Your second homework assignment is to tell yourself three times a day that you love yourself. Say the words out loud—"I love myself" or "I love you" (thinking of yourself as the "you" in this statement). It is especially meaningful to say it to yourself while looking at yourself in the mirror. Try this out. Saying "I love you" to yourself is a good way to start the day, since it affirms the attitude toward yourself that you want to maintain all day. As you say the words, get in touch with the feelings of love for yourself that you are cultivating. You may feel silly saying that you love yourself, but other people only put this down because they are so uncomfortable with it themselves. Assert your right to love yourself! Saying these words may bring other thoughts to mind, like "I hate myself" or "I don't deserve anything good," but continue saying "I love myself" anyway, and don't give up. You will change.

Don't let another day go by without starting to love yourself better. You deserve your love and care. Start today telling yourself that you love you and doing nice things for yourself. You'll love yourself for it!

Step 9

You're Not Perfect But You're Perfectly Good Enough

We set up harsh and unkind rules against ourselves. No one is born without faults.

—Horace

Most of the self-criticisms and self-put-downs that we engage in (and that keep our self-esteem low) occur as a result of thinking that we have failed to meet a standard—that in some way we are not good enough because we have not done something well enough or we have not pleased someone.

If we think that we are not good enough, we have been judging ourselves against the wrong standards. We are "good enough" right now! Remember, we are not OK, no one else is OK, and that's OK.

"Standards" and "rules" are guidelines that we use to tell us when our behavior is OK and when our behavior is leading us in a productive direction. If your standard for yourself in schoolwork is that you get grades of "A," then you will feel OK and will feel that you have met your standard when you receive an "A," but if you get a lower grade you may feel shame, guilt, and/or lowered self-esteem for failing to meet your standard.

Why do we need standards and rules? To a significant degree we human beings guide our behavior by thought and prediction, rather than by acting on instinct or without thinking. We choose behaviors based on our predictions of the outcomes of those behaviors (even when we are not conscious of our process of prediction). It is not possible for each of us to know all of the many possible outcomes of our behaviors, and analyzing all of the possible outcomes can take too much time, so we have constructed standards and rules to give us guidance on how to behave in different situations. They help us to control our behavior and stay safe, as well as identifying for us the behaviors that are likely to result in the most beneficial outcomes. The rule "don't leave your clothes on the floor when you take them off at night" tells you one way that you can avoid mother's anger. The standard "be nice to others" helps us to avoid negative reactions in general and encourages positive reactions from others.

Most of our standards for ourselves are based on trying to get the reactions we want from others—generally to keep important others, such as parents, happy with us. Many of these standards are given to us by parents, and we create some ourselves as our own guide to ourselves for how to get the reactions we want from parents or others. Standards are also set by societal institutions, such as church, school, and state. It will be important for you to examine all of these standards as you determine what standards you really believe in and what standards are good for you and for all people. What standards and expectations do you think you have to live up to?

Some standards are inappropriate and harmful, and you must learn to recognize them. It may be that a standard was an inappropriate one to begin with, such as "if you don't keep mother happy, then you are bad (and should feel bad about yourself)," or "if you are not perfect, then you are not good enough (and should feel bad about yourself)." Problems also result when as adults we keep a standard that was appropriate for us as children but is not appropriate for us now as adults, such as "don't ever talk back to dad, because that would be disrespectful," or when we inappropriately generalize a standard, such as translating "don't ever talk back to dad, because that would be disrespectful" into "don't ever talk back to anyone, because that would be disrespectful." In order to have healthy self-esteem, it is particularly important to reject the inappropriate standards of

(1) keep others from feeling bad even at the expense of your self-esteem,
(2) in order to be acceptable, you must be perfect, and
(3) anyone can achieve anything he or she wants to with enough hard work.

Some other examples of inappropriate and harmful standards and rules are—

❖If _____ is unhappy, then you have been "bad."

❖If my father (or mother, minister, teacher, etc.) said it, then it has to be right, and I must conform to it.
❖The stronger person gets to say what's right.
❖Since I am older, stronger, etc., I get more than you.
❖Since I am better than you, I get more than you.
❖We expect more of you than we do of the other children.
❖If a woman isn't married and has no children, then she is a failure.
❖If you don't go to college, then you are not as good as people who do.
❖Do whatever you feel like.
❖Get as much pleasure as you can now—you can worry about the future later.
❖You'll get more in life by taking advantage of others as much as you can.
❖It's OK to lie and deceive to get what you want.
❖If a different behavior on your part could have changed the outcome, then what happened is definitely your fault.

Do you understand why each of these standards is destructive, either to your self-esteem or to the welfare and self-esteem of others? If you're not sure, then you are probably hurting others or being hurt by it yourself.

In order to deal with problems regarding standards we must free ourselves from inappropriate standards we have held for ourselves, and we must determine our own appropriate, reasonable, and humane standards for ourselves, instead of accepting others' standards for us without determining for ourselves whether they are appropriate.

Standards are Relative and Fallible

Standards that are created by human beings are by definition fallible and subject to error. Unfortunately those who determine standards sometimes fall prey to a human tendency to set up rules and standards that favor themselves at the expense of everyone else. This can occur within a family or between different groups in society (Republicans and Democrats, conservatives and liberals, any majority versus any minority, etc.). Standards that benefit one group but have an inappropriate cost to others are immoral and should be changed.

Just because someone in authority states a rule or standard does not mean that it is appropriate or correct. Legislatures can make "wrong" laws, just as fathers can be unfair and pastors can misinterpret the Bible. The belief of some that certain standards are infallible since they come directly from God will not be addressed here, since it is a matter of individual belief, but the history of religion demonstrates clearly enough that there have been times when men claimed that a rule was from God simply to give divine weight to a rule that they wanted to establish themselves.

You can often tell when a standard is self-serving by the fact that a rationalization is given to justify it. When a mother makes her daughter baby-sit for the younger children because she doesn't want to pay a babysitter, she may pretend that it is a reasonable expectation by saying, "All teenagers should baby-sit—it will be good experience for you." This may be true, but the truth is that she is making her daughter baby-sit for her own benefit and not for her daughter's benefit.

As children we learn our standards from what our parents want and how they react, but as we learn more about the world, we discover major differences in standards, between different religions, different cultures, etc. Awareness of these differences should cause us to conclude either that we are right and everyone else is wrong (a position that some people actually take), or, more usefully, that the standards in question are human constructions and are therefore not primarily "right" or "wrong" but are rather either useful or not useful. Thus freed from believing that what we have been taught is automatically sacred and can never be changed, we can examine standards to see how useful or harmful they are, and we can even consider constructing better standards than those handed to us by others, particularly in terms of what we "expect" of ourselves.

The Inappropriate Standard of Being Perfect

Perfectionism is one of the most destructive standards one can have for oneself, since it guarantees failure. We imperfect human beings will never be perfect!

Children who think they must be perfect "know" that they are not acceptable to their parents the way they are, and they imagine that their parents would accept them if they were perfect. Occasionally a child will strive for perfection because parental expectations are so complex or vague that the child thinks that it would be simpler to strive for perfection than to figure out what the parents want. Being perfect would surely be good enough!

Unfortunately it is unlikely that parents who want perfection will ever accept a child, no matter how well the child performs. This withholding of acceptance may be rationalized as "motivating" the child to try harder, but it more likely expresses the parents' anger that they themselves were not accepted by their parents.

Those who have been trying to be perfect will have to accept the bitter truth that they cannot be perfect, and that being perfect would not in fact get them the acceptance they want so badly. You will have to do without the acceptance of those who cannot accept you, realizing that they do not accept you because of their own problems, and not because you are unacceptable. Letting go of this quest for unattainable acceptance usually brings tears, but it also brings relief. Accept yourself completely—it will feel so much better than berating yourself for not being good enough to merit the acceptance of someone else.

The Inappropriate Standard of Keeping Others From Feeling Bad

Some children learn that they are expected to suppress, repress, or reject their own thoughts, feelings, and needs so that others can avoid having unpleasant feelings themselves. This is usually accompanied by the belief that we "cause" other people's feelings and are therefore responsible for their feelings. It is important to correct these two errors if we are to take charge of our own standards and set humane, realistic standards for ourselves.

People have a tendency to blame their unpleasant feelings on others, rather than taking responsibility themselves for managing their feelings, and this blaming provides leverage in trying to get other people to change their behavior so that we will not have to feel our own unpleasant feelings. If mother is "sensitive" and can't stand any anger and sometimes reacts to anger with fainting spells, and the rule is established in the family that no one can express anger in her presence, then the children will probably feel that they are "bad" if they express anger in her presence, and it is quite possible that they will conclude that their anger itself is "bad" and that they are "bad" if they feel anger, even if they do not express it. They are likely to believe that their anger "causes" Mother's pain. Since it is natural for us to feel anger from time to time, and it is usually healthier to accept one's anger than to deny it, the development of these children will be harmed, and they will have an extra, built-in "reason" to feel bad about themselves for simply being normal human beings. It would be better for the children if the expectation or standard were that as the adult, Mother is responsible for doing something about her over-reaction to anger, rather than expecting her children to repress their feelings at the risk of harm to themselves.

How To Determine Who Is Responsible For a Person's Feelings

People are often confused about who is "responsible" for their feelings. In every situation there is a stimulus followed by our feeling reaction. The stimulus can be from within ourselves (like remembering something frightening that happened) or from outside (seeing an angry dog). If the stimulus is from inside ourselves, then it is reasonably clear that we are responsible for our feeling reaction to it, but when the stimulus is from outside, it is less clear which is responsible—the outside stimulus, or our own response. In our example above, the mother could say that having others express anger in her presence "causes" her distress and fainting, but Mother's over-reaction to anger is equally involved. If others did not express anger around her, she wouldn't feel bad, but it is just as true that if she didn't over-react to anger, she wouldn't feel bad either.

In order to sort out this confusion, a culture defines standards for various situations. In our culture, in general it is accepted that people are responsible for their own feeling reactions to outside things (unless an outside person has tried on purpose to cause them pain). In our example, since it is natural for people to feel and express anger, and since we expect people to be responsible for their own feeling reactions to things, Mother is seen as the cause of her problem, rather than the others who express anger in her presence. The children's anger is the stimulus that triggers her response, but their anger is not responsible for her response. In general, we say that no one can by themselves "make" someone else feel bad.

We usually take intent into account as well as impact. If a child, knowing that his mother over-reacts to anger, purposely displays anger in her presence, intending to cause her pain, then he bears some responsibility for the resulting pain. One's intent and having some idea of the likely results of one's behavior both create some degree of responsibility. It may be true that no one can "make" someone else feel bad, but if they want to make someone else feel bad, and they try to cause the person to feel bad, then they bear some responsibility if the person feels bad.

No matter what you do, someone can be upset with it, so we use the culture's standards of what is reasonable to decide who is responsible. As long as your behavior is within these cultural bounds, you are entitled to feel OK about your behavior. Sometimes a family will have different standards than the culture in general, in which case you must decide whether to accept your family's standard or the culture's standard. One way to check on whether another person's reaction to you is a unique, personal reaction or whether you are violating a widely held standard of the culture is to see whether all other people react the same way to that same behavior on your part.

As another example, if you are rude to others, then since rude behavior is not generally acceptable, it is not appropriate for you to say you bear no responsibility for the results of your rudeness. On the other hand, if your brother views any questioning of his behavior as rudeness, even when it is done politely and respectfully, then he is distorting reality. Your polite, questioning behavior was not rude. He has the problem.

Children are not usually in a position to reject their parent's incorrect accusations that they have caused the parent's bad feelings, but as adults we can dispute this and can refuse to take responsibility for someone else's feelings (as long as we are acting "reasonably" according to our general cultural standards).

The fact that someone is upset does not by itself prove that you have done something wrong. The question of who is responsible is determined by what most people in the culture view as reasonable and appropriate. It is essential for your emotional health as well as your self-esteem that you learn how to distinguish when you have some responsibility for another person's feelings (when you have acted inappropriately or have intended to cause emotional pain) and when you do not have that responsibility.

Take time to examine every situation in which you feel bad when someone else feels bad or in which another person says you "made" them feel bad. Decide whether your behavior was outide the usual cultural norms, and be honest about whether you wanted the person to feel bad. If neither was the case, then you are not responsible and do not need to feel bad about it.

The Inappropriate Standard That Anyone Can Achieve Anything If He/She Tries Hard Enough

Because we have a culture built on big dreams, we sometimes assert that anyone can achieve anything he or she wants just by working hard enough and trying hard enough. We would like to believe this in order to encourage ourselves to keep on working and to take some risks. However, logically it is just not true. A person who does not have the basic physical or intellectual capacity to do a given job will never do well at that job, no matter how hard he tries. Very few people who want to be president of the country will ever be president of the country, even if they are qualified, no matter how hard they try. We would do better to encourage risk-taking and to praise hard work, while not blaming those who fail by saying that they could have succeeded if they had tried harder. Sometimes people could have succeeded by trying harder, but sometimes they could not have.

Reject and Change Inappropriate Standards

If we continue to live by inappropriate standards, it is usually because we fear that if we disobey, we will be punished by the original givers of those standards, who seemed like gods with infinite power to us as children. We must accept that parents cannot hurt us now in life-threatening ways and that we are adults now and can survive and take care of ourselves, even if our parents (or some others) reject us. We may also continue to follow harmful standards because we don't want to "cause" pain to the givers of those standards by not following their rules. As noted above, our parents are responsible for their own feelings, as long as we are acting appropriately and reasonably. In the choice between not "causing" them any pain and seeking better self-esteem by rejecting their inappropriate standards for you, your self-esteem is a far more important and worthy cause. You can reject their inappropriate standards in a nice and respectful way, and you do not have to fight with others about standards—you can say what you no longer believe and what you refuse to do any longer, calmly and forcefully, and then stick to it, no matter what others say or do.

You may fear that if others were upset with you for not going along with their standards and expectations, you would automatically feel bad about yourself. We have noted above that just because someone is upset does not mean that you have done something wrong. It is crucial to train yourself <u>not</u> to feel bad just because someone else is upset or claims that you did not meet certain standards that are inappropriate or harmful for you. <u>You</u> should decide what standards you will follow. You may decide to change your own standards for yourself as a result of thinking through a situation, but the important point is that <u>you</u> are making that decision.

Exercise your right to independence by questioning <u>all</u> standards, rules, and expectations. Think about them until you understand why they were established as they are. Ask who benefits from the rule or standard in question, and who pays a price. Determine to your satisfaction whether it is an appropriate and fair standard or rule, or an inappropriate and unfair one. Think whether you would have established the rule or standard in that way or in some other way. After evaluating a standard, you may decide to follow it, or you may decide to revise it to work better.

There are some principles for evaluating the appropriateness and usefulness of a rule or standard. An appropriate rule or standard applies to everyone equally and does not put unfair burdens only on certain individuals. If there is a rule in the house that you turn out the lights when you vacate a room, then that rule should apply equally to everyone—all the children and all the adults—and not just to the children, and not just to the family scapegoat.

A rule or standard should be clear and readily understandable. Obviously people should not be held accountable for rules and standards they cannot even understand, except when extremes of societal danger are involved, such as murder or assault.

An appropriate rule or standard is relatively objective—that is, most people, once they understood the rule or standard, could tell whether it had been upheld or broken (instead of only the person who made the rule or standard being able to make that judgment—often in ways that are not clear or understandable to others). "Be home by midnight" makes clear what a violation would be. "Don't come home so late that I get upset" is an example of a standard that only the person who gives it can interpret.

The behavior prescribed by a standard should be appropriate to the developmental level of those to whom it applies. Requiring a child of six to make complex judgments involving adult-level social mores is clearly inappropriate, just as is making a child of six responsible for her younger siblings' behavior.

The purpose of an appropriate rule or standard is a legitimate, agreed-upon social purpose. If Mother is superstitious and believes that it is bad luck to wash clothes on Sunday, she might make a rule of no clothes washing on Sunday. There would be no legitimate social purpose to that rule, since its only purpose is a personal one—to keep Mother from worrying. Participating in this kind of irrational rule tends to make others a bit more crazy as well. On the other hand, a rule of no work on Sunday by anyone in the family, to conform to the family's shared religious beliefs, could be considered to have a legitimate social purpose (promoting the integration of the family through their religious beliefs).

A rule or standard should not ask more of anyone than is necessary in order to accomplish the purpose of the standard. If the intent is to motivate the children to do as well in school as they can, then the rule should not be "get all A's." It should be set reasonably according to each child's actual abilities. The recent movement among child advocates to establish a standard that prohibits any physical discipline of children requires more than is necessary to accomplish the purpose intended (to prevent actual child abuse), since it is not necessary to prohibit the many parents who can appropriately administer physical discipline from using physical discipline (such as a spanking with the open hand on the backside of a child) just so we can get those parents who cannot appropriately do this to stop going too far. The job of parents who can appropriately discipline physically is made much harder by this "standard" in order to get other parents who cannot control themselves to stop their inappropriate behavior.

The consequence or punishment for breaking a rule or standard should be commensurate with what is at stake. You shouldn't get five years in prison for your first traffic ticket, and a child who forgets to turn out the lights when he leaves the room should not be confined to his room for an entire evening as a punishment. Punishment for burning down the house would appropriately be much more severe, even if the burning was not intentional, because of the seriousness of the behavior and the danger to others.

The consequence or punishment for breaking a rule or standard should be within the bounds of what is humanly and culturally appropriate. Consequences are inappropriate when they traumatize a person or when they cause serious later damage to personality or self-esteem. A parent hurting his daughter's genitals as a punishment would be totally inappropriate, regardless of the offense, and any punishment that involves harming a person's self-esteem (for instance, by inappropriate or excessive put-down's and criticisms) is also inappropriate and should not be done. The judgment about what is appropriate calls on us to exercise our sense of fairness, rightness, and justice.

As an example, let's consider a family rule that specifies that one particular child always gets less than the others. This child (usually a disfavored child or a scapegoat) gets his ice cream after everyone else, when there always seems to be only a smaller portion left. Parents make promises to the kids, and they remember and honor their promises to the other children but always seem to "forget" their promises to the one left out or to have "reasons" why they could not carry those promises out. This child will end up with a feeling of inferiority and with lower self-esteem then if he had been treated as an equal. This standard is inappropriate because the rule specifies unequal treatment of those who should be treated equally. The rule is hidden (and denied by the parents), so that only the parents know why they are punishing or depriving the child. The purpose of the rule is socially inappropriate, since that purpose is to gratify some anger or hunger for revenge on the part of the parents. The consequences of the rule are inappropriate, since they unfairly harm the self-esteem of the child.

If you determine a rule or standard to be fair and appropriate, then you follow it because it is useful. If you believe it to be unfair and inappropriate, you can reject it and/or work to change it. When enough African Americans became convinced that society's discriminatory rules were unfair and inappropriate and also felt that change was possible, they moved to change them, with publicity-creating civil disobedience and court challenges to the laws. They openly made known their disagreement, and in whatever ways they could, they stopped following the inappropriate rules. Similarly, when you become convinced, as an adult, that some rules and standards are unfair and inappropriate (your parents', your own, or those of some institution), you can state your disagreement and seek change.

A child's power to change parental standards is of course very limited. A child can voice his opinion and disagreement, to whatever degree it is safe to do so, and she can suggest new rules and standards that would be more humane and fair, but parents may simply ignore the child. Probably the best that a child can do is to understand the unfairness of the situation and refuse to buy into the intended power or self-esteem implications of the standard. This means that every time the parent calls on the child to follow the inappropriate rule or standard, the child thinks to himself that doing so does not make him inferior or of lower value, even though his parents act like it does. To do this effectively would mean letting go to some degree of his need for parental approval and affirmation, and perhaps having a lower degree of respect for his parents, which would certainly be difficult and conflictful for a child to do.

As an adult, if you wish to change the rule that you get less than your siblings in the family, you can state your disagreement whenever inequities occur and insist on a fair share of things. You can discuss it with your parents, pointing out the many times (and the pattern) that you have received less than the others, and voicing the hurt you have felt because of this. You can request that this pattern be changed. You do not allow them to talk you out of your perception, because you have thought about it carefully and are certain of what has been happening. Every time it happens again, you point out what is happening, so that it becomes undeniably clear to everyone.

If discussing it, making clear what is happening, and requesting change do not work, then you must decide on your conditions for continuing the relationship. You are unfairly being disrespected and given an inferior position with respect to others, and you must decide what you are going to do about it, since to accept inappropriate standards that define you as inferior will inevitably lead to worse self-esteem. In some cases you can refuse to follow the inappropriate standard. In situations in which refusing to comply would lead to harsh punishments, you may voice your disagreement loudly but continue behaviorally to conform to the old standard. In some cases refusing to comply can lead to breaks in relationships, as when parents reject you if you will no longer submit to their unfair criticisms. It is almost always better for you in the long run to withdraw from those relationships rather than to let yourself continue to be defined as inferior as the price of preserving those relationships.

Before ending a relationship with someone who will not treat you appropriately, you can say to them that because you are a valuable person, equal to them and deserving of respect, the price to them of your company and relationship is that they will treat you as a valued equal, deserving of respect. For most people with poor self-esteem this is a startling concept—that other people must earn your company and relationship by treating you in acceptable ways, but it is a very important concept for improving your self-esteem. You deserve equal and appropriate treatment.

Choose Reasonable and Humane Standards For Yourself

Once you have freed yourself from unthinking slavery to the standards, rules, expectations, and reactions of others, you are in charge of choosing standards and expectations for yourself that will be humane, fair, objective, compassionate, realistic, and reasonable. In some cases, as above, you will be altering existing standards to be more reasonable and humane, as when you reject the standard of "be perfect" and adopt the standard of "honestly do the best you can." In other cases you will be mapping out new territory, as in the case of a woman deciding which of her new options are acceptable after rejecting the narrow expectation of her family that she must marry and have children right away.

Apply to your new standards the tests listed above, until you are sure that your standards are appropriate. Construct your new standards to maximize your happiness and that of others, by choosing standards that take everyone's feelings and well-being into account fairly.

In choosing more humane and reasonable standards, you may feel at first that you are "lowering" your standards. In fact, you are not lowering your standards but making them better and acknowledging that you have been harming yourself by demanding more of yourself than was appropriate.

Since as human beings we will inevitably require ourselves to meet some standard in order to think that we "deserve" to feel good about ourselves, it is necessary to know what a reasonable minimum standard is. You are entitled to feel good about yourself and satisfied with yourself if

(1) you have made use of your abilities with reasonable effort and diligence in trying to support and take care of yourself (and those who are legitimately dependent on you, such as your children), and

(2) you have treated yourself and others decently and fairly and have not knowingly harmed yourself or others.

Note that these standards do not require succeeding at any defined level, but require only that you have honestly tried your best.

Any standards that require less than these two standards are immoral. Any standards that ask for more than these standards or ask you to break these standards is either immoral or asking you to sacrifice yourself for someone else's gain. Women who vie for status with each other by quoting their husband's incomes and putting others down on this basis are acting immorally. Parents who pressure their children to get better grades than the neighbor children should ask themselves why they are dissatisfied with themselves and want their children to make them feel better. This is not an argument against aspirations, goals, and ideals. It is fine to aspire for and hope for goals beyond these two baseline standards, but goals and aspirations beyond these baseline standards should never become a reason for criticizing yourself, putting yourself down, or lowering your self-esteem.

Examine all of the standards that you are trying to meet and live by, regardless of their source, to determine if some are unfair and inappropriate. Reject and revise any that are unfair and inappropriate, and make them appropriate, reasonable, realistic, and humane. Use your new sense of what is fair and appropriate to question all inappropriate standards and expectations and to insist on equal and appropriate treatment from others.

Step 10

Do What Is Truly Best For You

This above all: to thine own self be true.
—William Shakespeare

Everyone has a right to his own course of action.
—Moliere

Because as children we have to learn a complicated set of rules and standards for our behavior, many of us have developed a habit of checking on ourselves every few minutes to see if we are doing the right thing. Some people do this checking in a suspicious, angry, and aggressive way, always looking for something to criticize. When we find that we are not meeting standards or are about to do something wrong, we punish ourselves or scare ourselves away from doing "wrong" behaviors, with painful feelings such as fear, shame, guilt, or feeling as if we are "bad," with attacks on ourselves that injure our self-esteem (self-criticisms and self-demeanment) and with deprivations and physical punishments. Making careful judgments about ourselves, others, and the world is natural and useful, including this process of checking and judging whether we are meeting standards or not, but when judgment takes on a harsh, suspicious, and critical tone, it becomes destructive, and you become your own enemy. Sometimes by this very process of harsh and punitive judgment about ourselves, we become dysfunctional and very unhappy people. (Those who do not develop much of a "conscience," of course, do not have this problem, since they rely on external punishments or the fear of those external punishments, to control their behavior.)

Harsh and unreasonable judgments are used as a method of self-control because as young children we must control ourselves by some method, but we don't yet understand enough about the world and the consequences of our behavior to make adaptive choices of what to do, and our neurological systems are not mature enough to easily control our own behavior. Once we become able to understand the reasons for the rules (how lamps are useful; how much they cost; how unhappy parents are when lamps are broken; etc.), we can govern our behavior by reference to these consequences, instead of depending on scaring and hurting ourselves. This is the basis for an alternative way of controlling your behavior—by doing what is going to be best for you!

Instead of harming or punishing yourself to control your behavior, "do what is best for yourself," based on all of the consequences of your behavior.

Some will fear that this method of self-control would not be self-control at all but would allow people to do what they felt like doing at the moment, resulting in much worse behavior than the more common methods of self-checking, self-punishment, and fear of external punishment, but doing what is truly best for you is not the same as doing what you feel like doing, or doing what gratifies your immediate desires. Neither is it doing what someone else thinks is best for you (such as your parents when they told you to do things that would be "good for you"). It is doing what you really think is best for you! This will result in you taking more responsibility for the consequences of your choices. You should not depend on others to tell you what to do, and you should not blame them when your decisions do not work out. You are responsible. Trying to do what is best for you will automatically make you want to do it right!

Determining What Is Truly Best for You

If doing what is best for you is going to produce good outcomes for you, it requires that you make good decisions about what to do. The primary reason for poor decisions about what to do is not taking into account all of the consequences of your chosen behavior, either through ignorance, carelessness, mistaken beliefs about outcomes, or trying to fool yourself into believing that you do not have to take certain things into account or that you will deal with those consequences later. You may wish to continue playing golf instead of going to meet your wife at the time you agreed to, and you think you can lie or make an excuse and put up with her immediate anger if you are late. If the long-term consequence, however, is destroying her trust in you, then you should carefully consider whether you want to do what you feel like doing right now (and damage her trust in you), or give up your current pleasure for the sake of keeping your marriage healthy.

This important aspect of maturity is called the ability to delay gratification, which means giving up a current outcome in order to work toward a more important outcome some time in the future, such as getting up every morning for the sake of one's paycheck next week, or living on less money while going to college, hoping to live better later on as a result of one's education.

People also make poor choices of behaviors by not taking into account the impact of their behavior on others (and the resulting impact of others on them as others react to that behavior). If we wish to cheat or deceive others in order to get what we want, we may hope that we can "get away with it," or we think that we would rather put off dealing with the possible consequences until some time in the future rather than being realistic about it now. However, in doing this we ignore how cheating and deceiving others will cause them to treat us. They will naturally be angry and try to get back at us. Our cheating and deceiving also changes the total social system in the direction of less trust and less love. We see around us examples of people who for a time do seem to "get away with it," but those people are not only harming certain other people directly, but they are also changing your future with their actions, as they tilt the overall balance of human interactions just a little more in the negative, distrustful direction. If we all did it their way, this would be an unpleasant and unhappy world indeed. (This is a good time to examine your own beliefs about what the best way is to make your life as good as you can. Will you be better off by trying to use any means, including mistreating and harming others, in order to make your life good, or will you be better off by treating others well at all times?)

The third reason people make poor decisions about behavior is that we deceive ourselves in order to trick ourselves into doing what we want to do, instead of being honest with ourselves about the predictable consequences of our behavior. If I want to invite only "popular" people to my party, and my best friend is not "popular," then many people in my position would rationalize not inviting my best friend, by thinking to themselves something like "He won't mind," or "He'll never find out." Of course, your best friend will mind not being invited to your party, and he will find out. By ignoring or altering in your own mind the truth about the predictable consequences, you end up making a bad choice of behavior.

"Doing what is best for us" requires that we have enough self-control to take time to recognize that what we first feel like doing may not be the best thing for us, as well as the self-control to refrain from doing what we first feel like doing while we choose our behavior carefully and do what we believe will be truly best for us.

If doing what you think is best for you often results in failure and pain, then you are causing bad outcomes for yourself, and you will come to doubt and hate yourself. Not doing what is truly best for yourself usually means that there is a part of yourself that insists on acting immaturely by ignoring the consequences of your actions, or there is part of you that wants you to suffer and fail. In either case, it is in your best interest to make some changes!

Once we understand what is best for us, in order to actually do it we must speak and act within ourselves with a unified voice. For most of us, there is a struggle between that part of us that weighs all of the consequences of our actions (the "adult" and more rational part), and another part of us that says that we should get all we can for ourselves right now, regardless of future consequences and regardless of how we may harm others (the "child" and more impulsive part). In order to act with a unified voice, the child part must come to trust that he is being taken care of in the most effective way possible. The impulsive, child part of us must come to trust that the more rational part really wants us to feel good, and the more rational part must reject all of the hypocritical ways in which parents or others tried to get us to "be good" by doing what they wanted us to do which was really for their benefit and not for our own. That impulsive part of us must come to believe that by exercising some intelligence and some control and by doing what is best for us, we will end up better off than if we simply try to get all we can for ourselves any way we can. This confidence allows the child to grow up, because he then believes that adult and mature ways will produce the best outcomes. (We must also become comfortable with sometimes giving up what we want right now in order to get more in the future.) In the meantime, you must comfort the child part of yourself as needed, and make sure that you do not deprive yourself (and the child part) so much that you provoke a further internal rebellion! Inner dialogues in which you get to know and become a friend to that "inner child" are quite useful in moving toward resolution of this conflict—see "Self-Parenting" by John Pollard.

Overcoming addictions presents another example of doing what is best for oneself. The most common addictions are to drugs, alcohol, or food, but we can think about addictions more generally as over-attachments—specifically over-attachment to anything that gives immediate pleasure. The problem with all damaging over-attachments is that the long-term negative consequences, which in most cases far outweigh the immediate positive consequences, are ignored in favor of immediate gratification, and we therefore do not do what is best for us in an overall sense.

The only consistently successful way to deal with addictions and over-attachments is to see, accept, and really believe that the negative consequences in fact do outweigh the positive and then to do what is best for yourself by refraining from the addiction or attachment. As you weigh the two courses of action, you have to feel the painful future consequences of the attachment as strongly as the immediate pleasurable ones, so that you can make a proper choice. You have to persevere in that choice of doing what is best for you long enough to see in tangible ways that it has in fact been better for you to refrain from the immediate pleasure. That realization or proof becomes the reinforcement that will make it easier at each succeeding choice point to make the choice for doing what is better for you.

Keeping a Clear Conscience

In order to do what is truly best for yourself, it is important not to violate the principles you believe in. We choose standards and principles that will make our lives as productive and safe as possible, so when you violate standards and expectations you believe in, you lose the guidance you should be getting from those standards, which makes you less safe and less productive—clearly not what is best for you. Violating your own chosen standards also tells you that you cannot trust yourself, and it suggests that you will probably be seen as untrustworthy by others. If you continue to violate your own standards, you will make bad decisions, you will come to look down on yourself, and your self-esteem will suffer.

In the traditional view of conscience, when we violate standards we feel guilt, shame, and/or fear of punishment. Fear of punishment usually ends when the punishment is received, but unresolved shame, guilt, and the feeling of being "bad," on the other hand, often cause us significant, ongoing inner problems. These feelings are painful, and they can preoccupy us so that we are unable to concentrate on living. Because it is so difficult for most of us to effectively process and rid ourselves of these particular feelings, it is much simpler not to arouse them in the first place. Hence the recommendation to keep a clear conscience.

Step 11

Treat Yourself Well

He who would be well taken care of must take care of himself.
—William Graham Sumner

If you feel good about yourself, then you will naturally treat yourself well, since you view yourself as deserving good treatment. And, in order to build and sustain positive self-esteem, it is absolutely essential to treat yourself well, so that you associate yourself with the good feelings resulting from how you treat yourself. Creating good outcomes for yourself is the simplest way of creating good self-esteem.

Being able to treat yourself well depends on how well you have adopted the elements of our program for improving self-esteem. In order to treat yourself well, you must be aware of your needs, and you must accept your needs. You must believe that you are deserving of good treatment. You must believe that you have the same right as anyone else to the good things available to you in life. You must believe that you are the equal of others. You must love yourself, since loving yourself is the primary motive power behind treating yourself well. You must have humane and reasonable standards for yourself and live by them consistently, or you will feel that you are such a failure that you do not deserve good treatment.

Meet Your Needs Acceptably

Meeting your needs well is one of the most basic ways of affirming your value and worth. Each time you choose not to meet your needs, you are confirming to yourself your lack of value and worth. Do you want to meet your needs, or do you neglect and punish yourself by not meeting your needs?

No matter how we try, we cannot always meet our needs, but if we try our best and are able to meet our needs acceptably much of the time, then we can accept not having our needs met occasionally. If you think that you have made reasonable efforts to meet your needs or have "done your best," then you can feel good about yourself for making those efforts, whether or not they resulted in the outcomes you desired. Neither is it necessary to meet your needs at higher than minimal levels in order to feel good about yourself. You can feel just as good about yourself for having a decent car and apartment as you can for having a Cadillac and a mansion.

While it is important to meet your needs acceptably, it is considerably less important (for self-esteem) to have your wants gratified. Needs, such as food, clothing, and shelter, are basic and essential. You may want lobster and a Mercedes, but you do not need them. Wants are discretionary, and the importance we place on them is up to us. In order to be reasonable in your expectations about your needs and wants, it is essential to be clear on your priorities!

Be Responsible and Trustworthy Toward Yourself

As the most important person in your life, you should be more responsible and trustworthy toward yourself than toward anyone else. If you are irresponsible with respect to yourself, then you will take actions that harm yourself. If you cannot trust yourself, then you will give up trying to take charge of your life, since you will expect that you will usually let yourself down or mess things up. In both cases, you will be very limited in your ability to create good outcomes for yourself.

If you treat yourself in untrustworthy and irresponsible ways because you feel that this is the normal way for you to be treated, or because it is consistent with your already established poor self-esteem, then work on believing that you deserve good treatment, make a conscious decision that you want to treat yourself better, and change your behavior. You will start noticing more (and disliking it more) when you act in untrustworthy or irresponsible ways toward yourself, and you will try consciously to change these patterns. It will help to purposely do one nice thing for yourself every day, and see what feelings that brings to the surface.

Do What Will Be Best For You and In Your Best Interest

Doing what is best for you and what is in your best interest are extremely valuable ways to treat yourself well. Since I have argued that you are already doing what you think is best for you (since it is impossible for human beings to do otherwise), if you are not doing what is actually best for you, it is essential to understand why you are choosing your actions poorly or believing that you deserve bad outcomes.

If you choose your actions in order to cause yourself pain or because you believe you don't deserve better, I invite you to continue to work on basic acceptance of yourself as a worthwhile and positive person. You deserve good things in life just as much as anyone else.

If you choose your actions poorly because you ignore the long-term consequences of your actions or your impact on others, then you must expand your view of what is in your best interest. (How to take into account all of the consequences of your behavior was described in Step 10.)

If you choose your actions poorly out of ignorance—because you do not understand yourself, others, or the world well enough to make accurate predictions regarding the outcomes and consequences of your actions, then it is in your best interest to open up your mind and learn more about yourself, other people, and the world. When you make inaccurate predictions about the consequences of your behaviors, think back over what you can learn from the mistakes, and alter your predictions so that you will be more accurate the next time. The more you learn, and the more wisdom you develop, the better able you will be to do what is best for yourself.

Stop Criticizing and Blaming Yourself

Many of us criticize and demean ourselves many times a day, which is one of the things that is most destructive to our self-esteem. We criticize and demean ourselves ("Boy, that was stupid," "You'll never get it right," "I'm just no good," "You're hopeless," etc.) because we believe that we "deserve it," since we are such failures, or because we use criticizing and demeaning ourselves as a method of keeping ourselves from doing bad things. Not only does this self-criticism hurt, but it is inappropriate and unnecessary. I have argued throughout this book that you are OK just the way you are, that you are not constantly failing, that you are "good enough," and that you are just as good as other people. You are in fact a wonderful and amazing being, and you were created or constructed to be positive and successful. It is not appropriate for you to harm yourself emotionally with constant criticism and blame. You must come to accept yourself as valuable, worthwhile, and deserving. Step 10 presented controlling your behavior by doing what is truly best for you as an effective and less painful alternative to criticizing and demeaning yourself.

Stop criticizing and blaming yourself. Notice whenever you criticize or blame yourself, and let your more rational self examine whether there is any justification for it. No matter what the circumstance, construct a supportive, accepting, but realistic statement to substitute for your criticism or blame, and make that statement to yourself. For example, instead of "You stupid moron; you should have known that you didn't have enough time to get to that appointment," say to yourself "I regret that I was late for that appointment, but I honestly didn't know that there would be that much traffic; next time I will make my life better by leaving a little earlier," or "I realize now that I didn't leave early enough for that appointment because I think I'm supposed to mess things up and be seen as inferior; this way of looking at myself is harming me, and I am going to do my best to change it." You will feel much better if you take a compassionate, understanding, and forgiving attitude toward yourself!

Respecting, accepting, and loving yourself are the most powerful positive behaviors you can do to improve your self-esteem, and stopping criticizing, demeaning, and rejecting yourself is the most powerful thing you can stop doing to improve your self-esteem!

Act Lovingly and Compassionately Toward Yourself

Another very important way to treat yourself well is to love yourself, which is the aspect of self-esteem that feels the best. Being affectionate and loving toward yourself means reacting to yourself with a loving perception, with a loving eye, a loving ear, and a loving "feel" for yourself. It means reacting to yourself from a loving observer's perspective.

Being affectionate and loving toward yourself means that you are kind to yourself, which includes being sympathetic, gentle, and forbearing. Being sympathetic toward yourself involves "feeling for" yourself in empathic and caring ways (while avoiding the unhealthy aspects of "feeling sorry for yourself"). Being gentle toward yourself means that you do not unnecessarily startle or upset yourself or cause yourself discomfort or pain. You act softly, considerately, and gently, with awareness of your feelings and needs. When we are tolerant, forbearing, and accepting, errors, frailties, and mistakes are seen as an inevitable part of being human and are therefore tolerated with good grace and acceptance. This does not mean abandoning standards, but simply that in a tolerant and forbearing world, mistakes and frailties are seen as inevitable, and since they cannot be eliminated or beaten out of us, it makes for a better life to accept them when they occur (and strive to do better), rather than to punish ourselves ever more harshly in hopes of eliminating them completely from our natures.

Adopt a loving and compassionate attitude toward yourself, and express your love and compassion for yourself in how you treat yourself.

Follow the suggestions in Step 8 to do one loving thing for yourself each day and to tell yourself three times a day that you love yourself. Keep a diary of the loving things you are going to do tomorrow and how they turned out. We all love to be loved, and loving yourself is one of the greatest gifts you can give yourself. (Reread Step 8 for more details on how to love yourself.)

Comfort Yourself

Comforting yourself when you need it is a key skill in treating yourself well and in being able to be relatively emotionally independent.

Being comforted helps us to experience our feelings of hurt and then to let them go, and it helps us to restore our sense of hope regarding the future. Many people are rejected when they seek comforting from caretakers, and they believe, therefore, that they do not deserve comforting. Without comforting, children may permanently associate their hurt and failure with themselves, leading directly to poor self-esteem.

Perhaps the most common image of comforting is a mother holding a child, stroking the child's head, patting the child on the back, and saying "There, there, it's OK; you're going to be all right." From infancy, we associate comfort most with soothing touch and a soothing tone of voice. As adults, talking with someone else about our feelings can allow us to feel understood and to receive sympathy, support, reassurance, and soothing, but we can also provide these things for ourselves.

Make use of the people available to you for comfort. Choose someone who seems like a nice person. Approach the person and let him or her know of your need for comforting, even if you would normally avoid letting anyone know you need something. You might say, "I would appreciate you letting me talk to you for a few minutes. I have been feeling really hurt (or upset, etc.) about something, and I think it would be comforting to me just to talk about it with you. Would that be OK?" Then tell the other person how what has happened is affecting you and your feelings. Stick to your feelings and your own experience, and don't focus on blaming someone else. With people you are close to already, you can even ask for some comforting physical contact, like a hug or a shoulder to lean on or cry on for a few minutes.

If you do not get the comfort you ask for, take it with good grace. You are not being denied comfort because there is something wrong with you or because you do not deserve it. You do deserve it. Try someone else next time. You will succeed if you keep trying.

Learn to comfort yourself by imitating others who have comforted you, and by imitating comfort you have observed being given and received by others. You can provide for yourself each of the elements of comforting—sympathy, feeling understood, support, reassurance, and soothing.

Be sympathetic and compassionate toward yourself. Let it be OK to feel hurt when you feel hurt, and respond with sympathy and compassion rather than by criticizing yourself and suppressing your feelings (even when your pain is due to a mistake of your own). Take your pain and your needs seriously, and do not demean or deny them.

Be understanding toward yourself. Accept your behavior and feelings. Look at the whole picture, and give yourself credit appropriately. Don't be quick to criticize.

Give yourself support by being there for yourself and by being able to count on yourself. Don't criticize yourself for needing support. Stand beside yourself with determination and strength, providing support to yourself that you can use to persist and to overcome obstacles before you. Make all of your abilities, capacities, and resources available to yourself, holding nothing back.

When we want comfort, we want to be reassured that things are going to be all right—that things will turn out in a way that we can live with. In providing reassurance for ourselves, a part of ourselves must be able to step back and see things somewhat objectively, even when the rest of us is in turmoil and therefore not seeing things clearly. Work on developing your capacity to see reality as it is, even when you are upset. Even if your internal state is a mess, your external situation is often not as bad as your feelings would suggest. (Naturally, the more we "catastrophize," or let our upset exaggerate the problems we face, the less able we will be to provide this more objective assessment for ourselves.)

Practice reassuring yourself. Try saying the words right now— "There, there, everything is going to be OK." Say them as if you were reassuring another person, but now the recipient is you. If you reject your own reassurance, ask yourself why. Are you saying you couldn't possibly believe yourself? Are you saying that what you have to give yourself is not worth having? Work on changing whatever is getting in the way so that you can receive and benefit from your own reassurance.

Soothing is acting so as to calm down the person being comforted, to calm her troubled emotions, to calm her crying, and so forth, so that her emotional state returns to a manageable equilibrium. The message in the words, "There, there, everything will be all right," is reassuring, but when the words are said in a soothing way, the emotional message is one of soothing. It is also soothing to most of us to take an action or be in a state that would normally be incompatible with being upset, such as being relaxed physically or eating something we like. This is why stroking the head of a person tends to be calming for him or her. It provides relaxation, which is incompatible with being upset. Being given milk and cookies can be soothing, because we focus on the good sensations of the milk and cookies, and our upset and concerns fade somewhat into the background.

We can also derive comfort from objects, activities, or sensations that we associate with comforting. Holding and looking at a picture of a loved one when distressed can feel comforting. Activities can be similarly comforting, such as the person who felt great comfort as a child in taking a walk with someone who provided comfort and now takes a walk alone or with someone else and through this feels those old feelings of comfort. Sensations, like a hot shower or eating, are often conditioned comforters as well. Develop your inventory of actions and objects that are soothing—such as eating a favorite treat, taking a walk, or holding your teddy bear, and use them to soothe yourself.

Developing your comfort sources and abilities will do you no good, of course, if you do not allow yourself comfort or if you do not believe that you deserve comfort. You must believe in your deservingness, and then use that belief to overcome any reluctance and fear that you have. If you were told "You're just feeling sorry for yourself" when you needed comforting, those people were trying to get away from your feelings themselves by telling you that your feelings were wrong. We must overcome this bad training by making it a "good" thing to feel sympathy and compassion for ourselves when we are hurt. If you feel that your own comforting is not enough, because you have always believed that what is inside you is by definition less valuable than what is inside others, you must reject this definition of yourself as having less worth and accept your own comforting as being just as valuable as comforting received from others.

As we have discussed before in other contexts, to believe that you deserve comfort may put you in touch with the pain of wanting comfort in the past and not being able to get it. You must go through that pain from the past in order to allow yourself to become able to have your feelings again and to treat yourself well.

Take Good Care of Yourself and Do Good Things for Yourself

Another way to treat yourself well is to take good care of yourself. Taking good care of someone else would involve such things as meeting that person's needs, paying attention to her when she needs something, being trustworthy and responsible toward her, ensuring her safety, and trying to contribute to her well-being, welfare, and happiness when possible. In taking good care of yourself, then, you would meet your needs acceptably or as well as you can within the limits of your situation. You would pay attention to yourself, so that you know what you are feeling and what you need. If you are taking good care of yourself, you would try to make your life better and happier by being trustworthy and responsible in your actions that affect your life.

If you take good care of yourself, you are concerned about your safety. If you take risks with your safety, it probably means either that you are unhappy enough that you need the thrill of danger to distract yourself from your existence, or that you do not consider yourself important enough to be worth protecting.

If you are taking good care of yourself, you wish to enhance your well-being, welfare, and happiness (in other words, to make your subjective experience of life as positive as it can reasonably be). You would be nice to yourself and kind to yourself. Above all you would love yourself and put that love into practice every moment that you possibly could.

Our consumer society tells us that we can be happy only if we have many possessions and spend our time in artificial experiences ("entertainment") that substitute for dealing with ourselves and with life directly by distracting us or trying to change our feelings through fantasy. The child's concept of happiness involves basically security and immediate pleasure, but as we mature, meaning, satisfaction, and fulfillment become as important as happiness in our efforts to have a good life. To achieve satisfaction and fulfillment one must make good use of one's abilities in a cause that has lasting meaning to one. These causes are expressions of our values and may be found in the areas of family, hobbies, art, politics, and social justice. It doesn't have to be complicated—there can be sufficient meaning and value in simply taking good care of ourselves (and those who are dependent on us) and being a good neighbor.

A good life includes a lifetime of doing good things for yourself, day in and day out. You must have a loving, positive attitude toward yourself, which inclines you to naturally think of what will be good for you or feel good to you and then do the work necessary to make these things happen. If you are feeling tense and exhausted by Thursday, but you can't let down completely because you must still work Friday, think to yourself about what you could do for yourself that would help—what you could do to take good care of yourself and to be nice to yourself. It occurs to you that eating out would be enjoyable and allow you a chance to relax, so you choose a restaurant and have a relaxing and tasty meal. You enjoy the meal and the variation in your routine, but just as important is the feeling that you are taking care of yourself. You cared about your feelings, and you did something about them, so you feel cared about.

Start practicing right now. Every day, take a few minutes to think of good things you could do for yourself, and plan for how you will proceed with those that are appropriate and feasible. You can't have everything you want—no one can, but you can do more for yourself than you have been doing (due to your poor self-esteem), and you will love yourself for doing it!

Step 12

Ensure That Others Treat You Well

I am treating you as my friend, asking you to share my present minuses in the hope that I can ask you to share my future pluses.
—Katherine Mansfield

In order for most people to maintain good self-esteem over the long term, it is important that they be treated reasonably well by others. Some exceptional people can maintain good self-esteem within themselves even though they are chronically treated unfairly or badly by others, but most of us need to have our value confirmed in the world from time to time in order to maintain our self-esteem. We are not in complete control of the behavior of others, of course, but this chapter will explain a number of things that you can do to get the best treatment you can from others

Even beyond learning to interact with others in ways that get you what you want, this chapter promotes expecting and demanding good treatment from others. For someone with poor self-esteem it might be unthinkable that you could successfully demand good treatment from others (or move on to seek better treatment from other people who can appreciate you more), but some other people value you more than you realize. You have no obligation to endure bad treatment from anyone, and everyone can be valuable to certain others in relationships.

Learn to Understand Others

In order to understand others as accurately as we can, it helps to consciously avoid several common sources of misunderstanding others. Some errors result from not attending adequately, due to feeling ashamed or inferior or being overly preoccupied with our internal self-criticisms and self-evaluations. These feelings may cause you not to be able to look directly at others and therefore not to be able to see what is really happening, or they may interfere with being able to take in what you are seeing. If you do not observe others closely and directly, because you are shy or feel inferior, because you feel so hurt by others that you cannot bear to focus on them, or because you are too preoccupied internally with feelings or conflicts, then naturally you will not gain the information that you need in order to understand others.

Another source of error is distortion due to emotions we are experiencing. When we are afraid of being hurt, disappointed with others, or angry with others, our feelings are likely to lead to distortions in how we see other people. It is a considerable challenge to see reality accurately while experiencing painful feelings, but you can train yourself to do this, by learning to comfort yourself and by refraining from trying to make yourself feel better by blaming or denigrating others.

Having accurate empathy for others is essential for living together harmoniously and productively. Empathy can be defined as the intuitive understanding of the experience of others through an imaginative recreation of their experience inside ourselves. Empathy is an extremely important human capacity, because it allows us to recognize our basic similarity to other people and therefore become willing to give them the same rights that we have. Empathy also helps us to anticipate the reactions of others to various behaviors we might choose to do, so that we can then choose behaviors that will be most to our advantage.

Empathy involves both an emotional and a cognitive component. We resonate with the other person's emotional expressions, and we also perceive the other person's situation and place ourselves in that situation in order to imagine what the other person is feeling or otherwise experiencing. In both cases, we must be willing to let ourselves experience what the other person is experiencing in order for our empathy to be accurate.

The typical difficulties in having accurate empathy are not wanting to feel the same painful or unpleasant feelings that the other person is feeling, assuming that others feel and think the same way we do about the world (which they do not), being afraid of being too close to others, not correctly perceiving another person's situation, and not being familiar with the feelings likely to be associated with that situation.

To the extent that you avoid your own painful feelings, you will tend to be blind to those same painful feelings in others. This requires working to become more tolerant of the full range of your feelings.

Some people fear that closeness will result in "engulfment" (the primitive fear that if one is close with someone, one will be taken in or taken over and completely controlled by that person). Engulfment fears may require psychotherapy if they are to be overcome. Some people fear closeness because they fear being hurt or rejected in a close relationship, which can be overcome by becoming more supportive and loving toward yourself, to help you tolerate the negative things that others can sometimes do.

In order to perceive accurately the situation of another person and that person's probable feelings in that situation, we must be willing to experience empathically situations that we might find distasteful and undesirable. We must also realize that others may feel differently about things than we do and not assume that they feel the same as we do. We imagine ourselves in their situation and note how we would feel, but we must then adjust our empathic understanding for the ways in which the other person is different from us. Taking differences into account is especially important with a person from another culture or background, since that person will almost certainly have different assumptions than we do about the meaning of events and about how people are expected to feel about them. The more ways in which the other person is different from us that we can take into account, the more accurate our empathy will be.

Make Good Use of Social Skills, Including Empathy

Social skills, including understanding others, empathy, communicating, being close, jointly working out relationship problems, forgiving, predicting how others will react to our behaviors, controlling our own behavior as needed, and helping others to feel good and to meet their own needs are all essential to living with others peacefully and productively. A comprehensive discussion of how to develop social skills is beyond the scope of this book, but there are many self-help books available on the topic, as well as many other books offering sound guidance about human relationships. A counselor can help, your church may provide help, and social skills groups may be available from various social agencies, colleges, or self-help groups.

Express Your Needs Effectively in a Social Context

You must bring those needs that you cannot meet yourself to the attention of others in a way that will move them to help you meet those needs. This can be as simple as "Please pass the ham," or as complicated as a discussion with your spouse about your sex life. Expressing your needs adaptively involves—

- knowing what your needs are
- being willing to speak up
- believing that you deserve and are worthy of help and response from others
- believing that your needs are just as important as those of others and that you deserve equal treatment
- expressing yourself clearly to others (communicating appropriate assertiveness)
- enough social sense to know what times are good for expressing your needs and what times are not
- a positive and productive attitude about how to integrate your needs with the simultaneous and sometimes competing needs of others
- the ability to wait and be patient
- persistence so that you do not let your needs be brushed aside and forgotten in the press of other events and others' needs, and flexibility enough to adjust what you would ideally like from others to what is practicable and realistic at the moment

Many of these skills are learned through being a good observer, developing your empathy skills, and being willing to see others realistically.

In order to motivate people to cooperate with us in meeting our needs, it is especially useful to develop the skill of choosing your goals so that others gain or "win" at the same time that you are getting what you want. Helping everyone involved to benefit requires empathy and willingness to compromise. (The other way of doing things—the power model of getting what you want regardless of what happens to others— almost always leads to distrust and bad feelings between people.)

A particularly important aspect of effectively expressing your needs is being appropriately assertive, which means using an appropriate amount of forcefulness and persistence in putting your needs forth to others. "Forcefulness" means putting forth your needs with a strength that indicates both the importance of your needs and your importance in the status hierarchy. Persistence means that you do not give up asserting your needs and insisting on your rights, unless it becomes clearly destructive to your interests to continue.

Some people express their needs too weakly, because they do not feel deserving and equal to others, and some people express their needs in an overly demanding or aggressive manner (because they feel superior to others, or because they do not feel deserving and equal to others and feel they must overcompensate). In order to express your needs effectively, you must comfortably and fully believe that you are deserving and basically equal to others.

Your assertions will not always get you what you want, which may call on you to compromise or wait for another opportunity to get what you want. What is at stake will also determine how persistent you feel you must be. It is very important not to give up when the issue is whether you have equal rights, but it may be advantageous to compromise on other, more specific desires. (There are many good books on the details of how to be successfully assertive-see the bibliography.)

Insist on Being Treated with Respect

If you are to improve and maintain your self-esteem, you must insist on being treated with respect by others—the kind of basic respect that every equal member of the group is entitled to. If you do not have this respect, your self-esteem will almost inevitably suffer since we generally feel humiliated or inferior when we are not respected appropriately. (See Step 6 on respecting yourself.)

Insist on being treated with basic respect, and challenge others whenever possible if they unreasonably withhold basic respect from you. This means speaking up and pointing out that you are not being treated with appropriate respect. ("It feels like you are ignoring me and my needs here, and I'd like some of your attention, too.") If others will not respond appropriately, then you may be better off leaving those relationships and finding other people who can respect you and treat you well. If you cannot get away from those who disrespect you, as a last resort you can fall back on maintaining your own self-respect while continuing to press for the respect of others. You can act (through voice, posture, and attitude) as if you were respected, even when others are not treating you with respect. Making your own self-respecting attitudes clear in your behavior tends to influence others to respect you in spite of themselves.

Insist on Being Treated as Fundamentally Equal to Others

The most important social battles have to do with our right to basic equality with others and our right to be ourselves. If there is no reason why you should get a smaller share than others in the family, but your parents insist on giving you a smaller share, you must challenge this if you are to have self-respect and healthy self-esteem. If you are denied rights guaranteed to everyone because someone doesn't like something about you, then you must challenge it if you are to have self-respect and healthy self-esteem. You are fundamentally equal to others, so speak up and challenge anyone and anything that attempts unfairly to make you unequal or inferior.

Alter Punishing Relationships in Accord with How You Want Them To Be

As an adult you are not obligated to take abuse or harm from anyone. Take what happens to you seriously and recognize abuse or harm that occurs. Prepare yourself for confronting the abuse or harm. Help the other person to understand how you are being harmed, and ask him/her to stop harming you. Be persistent in your efforts to change the relationship so the harm will stop. Change your own behavior in the relationship so that you are no longer accepting or putting up with the harm or abuse. This will put pressure on the other person to stop harming you in that way. If you cannot get the harm to stop, prepare to leave the relationship, for your own protection and for the sake of your self-esteem.

You have no obligation to take care of the feelings of those who hurt and harm you. As we have discussed, others are basically responsible for their own feelings.

It is natural for human beings to try to escape from harm, but people with poor self-esteem often do not try to get away. The factors that disrupt our natural inclination to get away from harm are things like not believing you deserve any better, feeling responsible for the feelings and welfare of those who are harming you, being afraid to "make waves," and fearing that if you did leave, things might be even worse (once again based on the assumption that no one could find you to be valuable and that you don't deserve any better).

The fear of making waves is rooted for most of us in the expectation that if we make a big noise or make demands on others, their shaming or punishing responses will cause us to feel ashamed or powerless or both. People who act superior to you count on the fact that there are many adults who will readily feel like children if the other person acts like a parent. However, you are an adult now, and no one has the right (not even your parents) to put you down by acting superior or claiming to be superior! We have equal rights as adults, and we have a right to speak up if those rights are being violated.

If you are surrounded by a family or community that will not change, and you have no way of leaving it and finding a more accepting environment, then you may have to live with some mistreatment for a while. Children are often in this position, since they are usually unable to leave their families. Clearly and firmly believing that you deserve the right to exist and to be yourself, that you are the equal of others, and that you have an equal right with others to good things available in life will help your self-concept and your self-feelings, but you will have to live with the painful difference between your inner beliefs and how others are treating you. You will have to live with feelings of anger or sadness from knowing that others do not treat you appropriately and that there is nothing you can do about it at the moment, but this is better than surrendering your self-esteem completely.

Seek and Develop New, More Supportive, Affirming, and Gratifying Relationships

You may assume that since you are worthless, you couldn't find any better relationships than the ones you have now, but I can assure you this is not true. You share a common humanity with everyone, since everyone has the same needs for respect, affirmation, acceptance, and love. There is a whole world out there of people who are just as sensitive and caring as you are and who will enjoy relating to you in a responsible and mutually giving way. If you are unfortunate enough to be surrounded by people who mistreat you, you must change your environment and find the kinds of people with whom you can have more satisfying relationships. They want to find you just as much as you want to find them!

Assert Your Worth and Value in Response to Cultural and Societal Attitudes Which Act Against Self-Esteem

In Part I—Chapter Five we discussed a number of cultural and societal attitudes which act against the self-esteem of certain individuals. Examples include the assumption in our society that women and people of other races are inferior to white males, as well as the false belief in every culture that having higher social status makes a person "better than" others lower in the status hierarchy. <u>Any</u> attitude or belief that defines one person or a group of persons as inferior to others, whether it is within a family or throughout a society, acts to degrade the self-esteem of the person or persons defined as inferior.

As a part of ensuring that you (and others) are treated well, it is important for you to resist and oppose attitudes and beliefs that place you or anyone else at a disadvantage with respect to inherent value and self-esteem. This means speaking out against such attitudes and beliefs, in our families, in our communities, in our nation, and in the community of nations. When others express such attitudes or beliefs, tell them—respectfully—that you disagree. Participate in the political process in order to oppose such attitudes and beliefs, in city councils, legislatures, and Congress. Refuse to buy products if their marketing is based on inviting you to feel superior to others, and refuse to be entertained by movies, books, etc, that support the subjugation of some people by others. Others may not like to have their selfish and oppressive attitudes and beliefs exposed, but tyranny that is not opposed may succeed in enslaving us all!

PART THREE

MAINTAINING POSITIVE
SELF-ESTEEM

Chapter 8

Enjoy Being Yourself
by Living with Integrity

Seek out that particular mental attitude which makes you feel most deeply and vitally alive, along with which comes the inner voice which says, "This is the real me," and when you have found that attitude, follow it.

—William James

It is good to be yourself, and it is perhaps the most satisfying thing in human experience to be fully yourself—fully in tune with yourself, and fully expressing yourself in the world.

The satisfaction of being fully yourself far exceeds the pleasures and satisfactions of consuming or possessing. It can come in many forms and can occur at almost any time—feeling pleasure in the awareness of your thinking, the awareness of your physical actions, the awareness of doing something nice for yourself, etc. You can enjoy your awareness of yourself in many if not all of the activities you engage in throughout the day. We have discussed at length how we deny ourselves good feelings about ourselves by applying inappropriate standards to ourselves and by assuming that we don't deserve to feel good. Don't let these self-harming errors spoil your enjoyment of being yourself!

Previous chapters have made clear the problems that arise from suppressing our real feelings and thoughts and from pretending to be someone other than who we really are. I have recommended recognizing the rejected and hidden parts of ourselves and consciously making all parts of our real selves acceptable to ourselves once again. To leave pretending and avoidance of self behind frees us to joyfully just be who we are, to live without self-rejection. If we can support ourselves with our good self-esteem, then the fact that others cannot accept certain aspects of us becomes a nuisance to be dealt with, rather than yet another crisis of identity and hurt feelings.

Our pleasure in being ourselves is maximized by living with integrity. The dictionary defines "integrity" as "an unimpaired condition: soundness; firm adherence to a code of especially moral or artistic values: incorruptibility; the quality or state of being complete or undivided: completeness." We respect people who live with integrity, who believe in themselves and are true to themselves and what they believe in. One of the consequences of not having integrity is losing respect for ourselves, which then lowers our self-esteem.

To be divided against oneself creates much pain and many problems. Whenever we react to ourselves with negative feelings, we are divided against ourselves and cannot possibly do the best that we can for ourselves. Integrity is often abandoned through hypocrisy or inconsistency. It would be a loss of integrity to say that you believed in loving and comforting yourself while at the same time criticizing and wounding yourself.

"Completeness" implies being a complete person, with all of our strengths and weaknesses, all of our wonderful and not so wonderful traits. "Completeness" would call for knowing oneself fully and completely and accepting it all, without having to divide oneself into "good" and "bad" parts. Any forced suppression of self (i.e., feeling forced not to be who we really are, as opposed to feeling that we are choosing freely from among the many satisfying ways that each of us can be) results in unhealthy incompleteness and resentment on our part.

"Firm adherence to a set of ... values" is necessary for integrity, and in this case you are the set of values that it is essential that you adhere to! You have a set of values about existence that indicates the relative importance of various activities, the purpose of life, and the rules that you believe should govern conduct between people. You are the living example of your values and the only one who can clearly and completely illustrate them and represent them in the world.

Having integrity means to stick to what you believe incorruptibly. If you have integrity, you do not change your stand or your beliefs just because someone else wants you to, or because it would be to your immediate advantage to do so. If you do not believe in stealing, and you are in a situation in which you could easily take someone's valuable property without being detected, you do not all of a sudden change your values and take the property, rationalizing that while most of the time you are against stealing, this opportunity is too good to pass up.

Paradoxically, it might seem that if you believed in stealing, then you could steal and still have integrity! However, as we have discussed before, if we harm others, somewhere inside us we empathically experience that harm, which harms ourselves.

Having integrity requires that we do not distort the truth for our own advantage. We view ourselves and others objectively, and we are not hypocritical—for example, criticizing others for drinking too much but attacking anyone who accurately points out that we drink too much.

Not having integrity, then, has to do largely with being false— denying the truth, pretending to ourselves or others, and being hypocritical. Our challenge is to face who we are and work toward accepting who we are, while at the same time expressing our true selves in the world and having the courage to face whatever rejection or hurt that we fear others will give us if they do not like who we are.

If you are living with integrity, when someone challenges your right to be yourself you will assert your rights and stand up for yourself, but it is difficult for us to have integrity when to do so puts us at risk of being rejected by a person or group that is important to us. It is possible, though, to feel good about yourself and to maintain your self-esteem at the same time that you please some people but not all people. You will come to accept that "you can't please everybody."

Standing on your own and being yourself, even when some others do not agree with you, is a tremendous success and a wonderful confidence-booster. Think about some of the situations in which you would like to be more yourself but hold back because of fear. Decide if you think it would be "wrong" to be yourself and if you would be harming anyone else by being yourself. Now that you feel more worthwhile and can be content just being yourself and being alone for a while when you encounter rejection, you are in a position to have greater integrity and to take some risks in expressing more of your true self in public.

A young woman who gives in to being who her mother wants her to be, to the exclusion of her true self, will face a chronic integrity crisis. A young man who believes in the dignity of all people but whose friends openly demean African-Americans faces an immediate integrity crisis. For both of these individuals to have integrity and respect themselves, they must stand up for their beliefs.

Being yourself with integrity is the crowning glory of your efforts to be yourself and to have good self-esteem. Having self-esteem is being yourself in ways that bring you good feelings just for being yourself and for what you do. Having personal integrity is expressing your true self in the world and being consistent with your beliefs and with who you really are. Being yourself fully and freely and feeling good about it is the most joyous possible state of the individual human being. Enjoy being yourself. Pay attention to the good outcomes you cause for yourself, and feel good about them. Enjoy being yourself as you do everything you do, and take pleasure in being yourself when you reflect on the good things you do for yourself.

Chapter 9

Help Others To Have Good Self-Esteem

The greatest good you can do for another is not just to share your riches, but to reveal to him his own.

—Benjamin Disraeli

You can help others to have good self-esteem by treating them in ways that promote self-esteem (treating them with basic respect, accepting them, etc.) and by demonstrating and modeling for others how you live the skills and attitudes needed for good self-esteem—being aware of yourself, being honest with yourself, believing in your essential self-esteem rights, respecting yourself, accepting yourself, liking and loving yourself, enjoying yourself, being satisfied with yourself, dealing with standards in healthy ways, living by the reasonable and humane standards you have chosen for yourself, treating yourself well, and ensuring that others treat you well.

Demonstrate Self-Esteem Principles in Your Life

Show others by how you live that it is a great thing to be a person! Give others the wonderful you that is inside! Demonstrate by how you live that you view things with your own independent mind and are not defined by what other people think and feel about you, and give others the right to be themselves also. Live as if you are basically valuable, regardless of how others value you. Show others what it is like to feel that it is really OK to be yourself. Acknowledge without defensiveness the things about you that you are not happy with.

Express your feelings even if at first you are self-conscious and embarrassed doing it. Embarrassment doesn't last long, and it doesn't harm us. Actually, you will find that since practically everyone feels embarrassment, when others know that you feel embarrassed, they can relate more easily to you!

In order to be honest, responsible, and trustworthy with others, you must be honest with yourself. Notice when you are tempted to distort the truth in order to make things better for yourself.

By your joyous use of all aspects of yourself in living, demonstrate that you have a perfect right to exist and to be yourself.

Act as if you are an equal, and demand an equal share. Reject all attempts by others to claim superiority over you.

Treat yourself with respect at all times, and demand basic respect from others. Accept yourself completely, and stop criticizing and demeaning yourself. Love yourself, and treat yourself in loving, compassionate ways every day.

Reject inappropriate standards and expectations, and set your own reasonable and humane standards for yourself.

Demonstrate for others that you can control your behavior for positive reasons (to do what is truly best for yourself and others), rather than only for negative reasons, such as to avoid punishment. Be compassionate and accepting toward yourself and others, instead of harshly judgmental and punitive.

Don't make others inappropriately responsible for your feelings. Refuse to take responsibility for the feelings of others (unless you have in fact caused the person harm inappropriately). Have an integrated and reasonable set of values with which to determine for yourself which behaviors are appropriate and which are not.

Treat yourself well at all times. Take good care of yourself, meet your needs, and do nice things for yourself every day.

Use empathy and other social skills to induce others to treat you well. Model healthy and respectful self-assertion. Insist on respectful and equal treatment from others. Reject bad treatment by others.

Show others that it is better to leave punishing relationships that you cannot improve than it is to continue to suffer in them.

Model being yourself with integrity, so that others can benefit from seeing someone perform this very meaningful and marvelous feat. It is the peak of good mental health to be able, with relatively little internal conflict, to love yourself, to have good self-esteem, to use all of your abilities in a socially responsible way in your quest to meet your needs, and to be yourself with integrity.

Treat Others in Ways that Encourage Self-Esteem

Help people to feel respected by recognizing and acknowledging them. Appreciate others and treat them as if they were valuable and worthwhile. Tell people what you like about them and about their behavior. It takes little energy to say good morning to people, to comment when they look nice, or to say thank you when they have done something for you. Don't hold back out of fear of embarrassment. Sharing what you feel can help others to realize that they are not alone.

Be positive whenever possible. A positive atmosphere supports the self-esteem of everyone around and reinforces the perception that life is positive and that those who are participating in it are positive, too. See the potential in others, so that your positive expectations will help them to move toward better self-esteem.

See others realistically, and accept them anyway! Whenever you encounter something about a person that you do not like, either let it be or consider how to communicate it or reinforce it in ways that will help the person to change, if he chooses to, rather than simply criticizing and attacking him.

Be willing to see the complex truth about people and their circumstances. Reserve judgment until you know all of the facts in a situation, instead of making up your mind from gossip or from newspaper headlines. Don't blame the victim, and don't assume that the way things are is the way they should be.

Treat others unfailingly with basic respect at all times. Honor every person's basic human rights, dignity, and equality regardless of the situation and even when they have hurt you or done something you don't like.

Accept others as persons, even if you do not accept all of their behavior. Accept the ways that others are different from you. Differences don't have to be threatening. You don't have to be like others to be OK—you are OK just the way you are. And others don't have to be like you to be OK, either.

Include everyone in "us". Monitor all of the effects of your loyalties to various groups, such as family, ethnic group, and nation, since all sub-grouping tends to make you see members of other groups as them and "different" from you and to create an "us" against "them" perception of reality. Every time you make others "different" from you, you tend to place their needs and their very existence at a lower value than your own.

Develop your capacity to love everyone sincerely and without hypocrisy. You can genuinely enjoy and find others fascinating, and show them that at every moment you are ready to engage in a positive, respectful, accepting, cooperative, and affectionately loving relationship with them.

Demonstrate that you support the right of everyone to exist, by treating the needs of all persons as important and by treating them all equally.

Be honest with others as well as trustworthy and responsible toward them, since these actions, especially when they are not to your immediate advantage, tell people that they can trust you and that you view their welfare as important.

Treat everyone as basically equal, whether you like the person or not. Make each person's needs as important as those of everyone else. Accept the right of everyone to whatever good things are possible.

Be fair and judicious in the standards you set and the expectations you have for others (and for yourself, too). Make your expectations reasonable, humane, clear, and appropriate to those to whom they apply. Think about what is really important in life, and construct your standard of "success" accordingly. If you do, your own honest thoughts will not be in accord with what our society holds out publicly as its values (fame, fortune, possessions, success, etc.), but do not be dismayed. Believe in what is really important and live your values. It is not particularly important that others are misled as to what is really important (or that they have a different idea about it). You will make your contribution by living your values sincerely and honestly.

Be compassionate and comforting when others need it. Be loving, kind, and gentle toward others. In manifesting your attitude of kindness toward the world, pay special attention to those who have suffered the most damage to their self-esteem.

Speak out against cultural and societal factors that create poor self-esteem, such as prejudice, scapegoating, damaging gender and child roles, and inappropriate values. You demonstrate integrity to others by being true to yourself and speaking up for your values when it counts and when it is not easy to do.

Societal Changes That Would Benefit Self-Esteem

In addition to our efforts to help other individuals to have better self-esteem, we can influence our society toward changing those factors that harm the self-esteem of many.

It is inevitable in human status hierarchies for those lower down the ladder to feel inferior, and in order to improve self-esteem in general, I am proposing that we educate adults to alter this habit and to feel equal instead. No one is "better" than anyone else. It is essential for adults to understand that they can feel equal to and just as good as those higher than them on the social status hierarchy, while at the same time recognizing and accepting the reason for the hierarchy (organizing society while minimizing overt conflict) and the reason to continue to do their assigned jobs, whatever the status level of those jobs. The helping professions, churches, and schools could do a great service by incorporating this new attitude and passing it on to their clients, members, and students.

Self-esteem in general could benefit from a healthier set of values in society. The weight that we put on wealth and possessions dooms most people to mediocre self-esteem at best. Valuing people for performing their various roles well, taking good care of themselves and their families, and treating everyone decently could bring us together and help all sincere, hard-working people to feel better about themselves.

The self-esteem of millions would benefit if labeling children as either "good" or "bad" were eradicated. All people produce both "good" and "bad" behavior, but no individual is totally "good" or "bad."

It would benefit us all if we reacted to people as whole persons, with all of their positive and negative qualities, behaviors, and potentials, instead of viewing them only in terms of their immediate behavior as it affects us right now.

Because we are so reluctant to admit that many things are outside of our control (and that we are therefore relatively helpless), human beings have a tendency to blame someone for whatever goes wrong. Whether we blame someone else or ourselves, this blame does a great deal of damage to self-esteem. It is appropriate, of course, for us all to be accountable for failing to meet appropriate, assigned responsibilities, but is inappropriate to blame someone else just so that we won't have to feel helpless or guilty ourselves. It would be a big step forward for our whole society if we could better accept our own responsibility for our lives and our relative helplessness in life, instead of blaming ourselves so we can feel more in control or blaming others so we can avoid unpleasant feelings. Maturity involves seeing reality clearly and taking responsibility for ourselves.

People need heroes and role models, but our society's degree of worship of those with fame and money devalues the lives of ordinary people and indicates that many of us are bored and unhappy with our lives and disappointed with ourselves. The qualities of love, compassion, steadfastness, fidelity, trustworthiness, and cooperativeness are the qualities that make for successful marriages, successful child-rearing, and enduringly successful economic ventures, but no one stands up publicly for these values. The effort, struggle, and dreams of every ordinary person are important and interesting and can be deeply satisfying and fulfilling. We are all the heroes of our own lives. If your life is boring, then you will get further by thinking seriously about restructuring your life and values than you will by trying to live through others.

As people feel more powerless in our increasingly complex society, they wish for more power so they can feel in control of their destinies. Our entertainment media are happy to supply these power fantasies (movies, electronic games, etc.), and this exposure to power solutions to problems encourages the belief that power is an acceptable way to solve problems. Historical experience, however, shows that the exercise of power may promote behavioral conformity for the shortrun, but it also divides people, humiliates them, controls their behavior against their will, sets them against each other, and leads routinely to war. Similarly, our society's emphasis on "winning" promotes an "us against them" viewpoint in society, in which those on our team are OK and those who compete against us are bad guys. This book is based on the premise that caring and cooperative solutions lead to better outcomes for everyone—greater self-esteem, greater security, greater human harmony, and longer, happier lives. The use of our resources and abilities to solve meaningful human problems is the only power worth praising. Any and every use of power to take from others or to get ahead of others unfairly is a crime against humanity and should be identified as such.

Societal attitudes that demean any group lead to worse self-esteem for that group. Women, children, and racial minority groups have all suffered in our society from these demeaning attitudes. We must all adopt and assert attitudes of basic respect, worth, and equality for all individuals, regardless of their condition or who they are.

In our society we assume that it is OK to try to sell products or services by trying to "make" others feel inferior or threaten their self-esteem. (If you don't have this product or this status symbol, or if you are not like us, then you are inferior.) Free speech rights are important, but in my opinion free speech that aims to harm another person should be subject to penalty, even if the penalty is only that everyone understands that it is wrong to do and negatively reinforces it every time it is seen to occur.

Because in our society we use the carrot of more material goods and comfort to get people to work harder, most families now believe that both parents must work in order to support the family. The result is less parental time with children, less opportunity for parents to convey clearly their love, beliefs, and values to children, and therefore less opportunity for children to gain good self-esteem. In reality, if we were willing to live with the standard of living of twenty years ago (which was not too bad!), one working parent could support the family. Politicians say that they support "family values," but how many politicians encourage parents to choose fewer hours of work and less pay so that they can spend more time with their children? We are trapped by our desires and by our view of "reality"!

Advertising and the practices of the medical industry tell us that we should not have to tolerate pain and that we should seek relief for any and all pain, but to do what is emotionally healthy is sometimes painful, at least for a time. It is more difficult to take charge of your self-esteem than it is to allow it to be determined by others. It is easier to keep quiet when others are demeaning people with their prejudices than it is to stand up for the rights of all to basic equality. *It is important for us all to promote the value and importance of dealing with emotional pain instead of avoiding it, since it is necessary for maintaining our self-esteem and a healthy society.*

As our jobs grow in complexity and demand higher and higher levels of skill and knowledge, as technology replaces more and more low skill workers with machines, and as globalization moves more low skill jobs overseas, our society is creating a larger and larger "underclass" of people who cannot compete and who therefore live on disability, welfare, or crime, with predictable consequences in terms of poor self-esteem, harmful substance use, and hostility toward everyone.

There are not enough jobs for everyone, and too many jobs that are available pay so little that those workers cannot afford transportation or health insurance for their children, again with predictable self-esteem consequences.

We are responsible for the way our economic system works, and it is essential that we recognize that in our current system, we can no longer expect everyone to find his or her own job, and we must move toward greater provision by society of work for those who for whatever reasons are not adequately competitive in the job market. This could be accomplished through government-supplied jobs, government-supported jobs in private firms, a much higher minimum wage, large tax incentives for private firms to make low skill, living wage jobs available, jobs that allow frequent absences (due to disability or medical reasons), or in other ways. In addition, many of those who are now supported by the government as disabled should be doing productive tasks to the limit of their ability (for the sake of everyone in society as well as for their own self-esteem), regardless of whether they can do these tasks full-time in a normal job environment. These alternatives are not popular now, due to our wish to believe that anyone who tries can succeed, but this belief was never true, and it is even less true now. For the sake of the integrity of our society, and for the sake of the self-esteem of those less competitive persons, we must change our attitudes and redesign our systems.

A system of support groups focusing on self-esteem would be helpful to many. These could be nationwide and could provide a place for like-minded people to give each other support in their efforts to improve their individual self-esteem, as well as to discuss ways to promote better conditions in society for self-esteem. This book would form a good basis for a study group, with discussion of a chapter each week. In California, Dr. James Henman's C.A.I.R. (Changing Attitudes In Recovery) groups focus heavily on self-esteem as the basis for advanced "recovery"—the self-change that is necessary after becoming abstinent with regard to a substance or other addiction, or after beginning to deal with how one's singular past (like being abused) has made one's personality maladaptive.

What You Can Do

The most effective thing that you can do to encourage good

self-esteem for all is to live your own daily life according to the principles and guidelines that will raise and maintain your own personal self-esteem. Once you have integrated those principles into your own life and have truly accepted the benefits and the costs of doing so, you will be a living example of the ideals you profess, and this will directly help others to feel better about themselves, because of how you treat them, and because of your modeling of these ideals and principles. Wouldn't it be wonderful if this could be the norm in our society?

Simply put, we must, in all circumstances, respect and basically accept others and treat them as essentially our equals. It may help to think of applying the "Golden Rule"—that is, to treat others, with respect to self-esteem conditions, as you would like them to treat you.

You can be "part of the solution" rather than "part of the problem" by deciding to live as one who promotes the opportunity for good self-esteem for all. Be aware of what goes on in your own community, and across the nation, in terms of the impact of business and political actions on self-esteem. Write letters to your newspaper pointing out problems and solutions. Use your vote to support equality and good treatment for all. Volunteer to help organizations that enhance the self-esteem of young people or other groups in society. Boycott businesses and entertainment that pander to inferiority and power motives. Choose a job that allows you maximum time with your children. Sponsor a self-esteem support group and keep it available and publicized, regardless of attendance ups and downs. But most of all, live by what you believe in!

PART FOUR

A FINAL REVIEW

Chapter 10

Review of Actions Crucial to Good Self-Esteem

Five minutes, just before going to sleep, given to a bit of directed imagination regarding achievement possibilities of the morrow, will steadily and increasingly bear fruit, particularly if all ideas of difficulty, worry or fear are resolutely ruled out and replaced by those of accomplishment and smiling courage.

—Frederick Pierce

Throughout this book, a number of key psychological mechanisms have been described that will help you with self-esteem problems (and with other emotional problems as well). Since some of these methods are radical and unusual in the psychological and self-help literature, they are summarized again here. The few but powerful self-esteem exercises that have been described for you in the book are also summarized here. Make a commitment to yourself to implement these beliefs, attitudes, and actions in your life, if you have not done so already!

Don't Automatically Agree With Anything Anyone Else Says. Use your own independent mind to decide what you think is true—especially when the subject is yourself.

Don't Let The Views And Opinions Of Others Define Or Limit You.
Others only have their own individual, limited, and usually biased viewpoints about you. You are so much more than what others think or feel about you. Even if others view you negatively and treat you badly, you are still OK, and you still retain your basic worth and value as a person.

Believe Without Question That You Are OK And That Nothing About You Is Causing Others To Treat You Badly When They Do. You did not and do not "deserve" bad treatment. No one does.

You Are Not Inferior To Anyone Else, And No One Has Any Right To Be Superior To You. In terms of being a person, no one is any better than anyone else. Those who try to be "better than" you are trying to manipulate you. Don't buy into this game.

Superficial And External Factors, Such As Appearance, Wealth, Power, And Achievements Do Not Make A Person Any "Better Than" Anyone Else. You are as good as everyone else. The only things that really matter are how you treat yourself, how you treat others, and what you contribute to the lives of others. Believe this, and become a "values radical"!

See Others For Who They Really Are. Many People Who Claim To Be Or Pretend To Be Superior Are Actually Suffering From Poor Self-Esteem.

You Are Lovable And Acceptable Just The Way You Are. No matter what you have done, no matter who you are, and no matter how others have treated you, you are lovable and acceptable as a person just the way you are right now.

Accept Yourself Totally. Accept everything about yourself, and stop demeaning yourself by dividing yourself into OK parts and not-OK parts.

Stop Criticizing And Rejecting Yourself. Love yourself instead!

Be Satisfied With Yourself. If Someone Says You Are Not Good Enough, They Are Using The Wrong Standards. You are "good enough" to successfully be yourself, just the way you are. You don't have to have wealth or status to be happy or satisfied. You can feel good about yourself if (1) you make reasonable efforts to take good care of yourself and of those who are legitimately dependent on you, and (2) you treat yourself and others decently and do not knowingly harm yourself or others.

You Have The Right To Be Treated With Respect And As Basically An Equal At All Times.

Your Needs And Feelings Are Just As Important As Those Of Anyone Else.

Feel Your Feelings And Your Pain. Your feelings are the core of you, and in order to be maximally functional, you must know and be able to manage every part of yourself, including your feelings.

Learn Not To Automatically Feel Bad When Someone Criticizes You Or Is Upset With You, But Evaluate For Yourself Whether You Have Anything To Feel Bad About.

Control Your Behavior By Doing What Is Best For You, Not By Criticizing, Punishing, And Rejecting Yourself.

Don't Take Responsibility Inappropriately For Others' Feelings. You Have No Obligation To Degrade Yourself Or To Remain In An Inferior Position Just So Someone Else Can Feel Better.

People are responsible for their own feelings (unless you have acted inappropriately according to the standards applicable to everyone in society, or you have deliberately tried to hurt them). Just because someone is upset doesn't mean that you have done anything wrong.

Find Out Who You Really Are, And Enjoy And Celebrate It.
Most people are afraid to be who they really are for fear that someone will be upset by it. You are wonderful and unique just the way you are. Get to know your real self and enjoy it!

Develop A Great Relationship With Yourself. Your Relationship With Yourself Is More Important To Improving And Maintaining Your Self-Esteem Than Your Relationships With Others. We must learn to love and nurture ourselves as the basic support for our self-esteem.

See Clearly How Others Have Contributed To Your Poor Self-Esteem. Even those whom you love and who were supposed to love you may have contributed significantly to your poor self-esteem. Most people rationalize away how loved ones hurt them. You can see the truth about them and still relate to those people if you wish to.

Leave Relationships With Others If They Cannot Stop Harming You And Your Self-Esteem. As an adult you can survive without those people who are harming you and your self-esteem, and you will be happier without them.

Be The Best Source Of Comfort And Support For Yourself. If you take the risks of being yourself and not giving up your self when others are upset with you, then you will need to be able to stand on your own, at least for brief periods, by providing support and nurturance for yourself. Learn to love, encourage, and support yourself, and enjoy it! Learn to be your own best friend and supporter.

Self-Esteem Exercises

The number of practical exercises that have been presented in this book is small, but they are powerful, and they are sufficient to give you practice in those things essential to achieving your self-esteem goals. If you have not done these exercises, copy these pages and carry them with you so that you can start practicing!

Understanding Your Self-Feelings

Take at least a minute to clear your mind. (It helps to close your eyes and get in a relaxed position physically.) Then focus your attention on a general sense on yourself overall. Try to sense how you feel in response to yourself. Let yourself take some time for various feelings to come up. You may not like some of them, but it is important to make an honest start in finding out how you really feel about you.

Are how you act and treat yourself consistent with how you truly feel about yourself? Do you try to make it look to others as if you respect yourself and feel valuable, when in fact inside you don't feel good about yourself?

Can you distinguish your total self-esteem from your evaluative self-esteem? Do you feel good about yourself in a general way? Do you nearly always feel that you have to be doing or achieving something, or giving a certain impression to others, in order to be OK?

What proportion of your good feelings about yourself is the result simply of you feeling good about yourself (unrelated to other people), and what proportion is due to you feeling good about yourself because someone else feels good about you?

What evaluative standards do you use to determine whether it is OK to feel good about yourself? Make a list of the most important ones. Try to identify where you got those standards.

How much of the time do you succeed in meeting these evaluative standards well enough that you are able to feel good about yourself from an ESE standpoint? How much of the time do you feel bad about yourself because of not meeting these standards? What specifically do you often end up feeling bad about?

Do you try to feel better about yourself by feeling "better than" others? How do you try to set yourself up as superior to others? Do you notice ways in which your attempts to feel superior result in conflicts with others?

Do you tend to blame things on others that are at least partly the result of your own choices and actions, in an effort not to feel bad about yourself? How do you usually do this—blowing up in anger, pulling rank, character assassination, scapegoating others, or other ways?

Exploring Parental Influences On Your Self-Esteem

Did your parents' reactions make you feel as if your needs and feelings were OK, or did their reactions frighten you and make you feel like hiding your needs and feelings so as to protect yourself?

Do you feel that just by being who you are you cause negative or disapproving reactions in others? What is there about you that is so bad that it causes these reactions? What three things about yourself are you most ashamed of or guilty about? How did your parents criticize you as a child? What did they say or do?

How are your feelings about yourself similar to the feelings your parents had about you? How are the ways you treat yourself now similar to the ways your parents treated you?

How are your feelings about yourself similar to the feelings your parents had about themselves? How are the ways you treat yourself now similar to the ways your parents treated themselves (especially in terms of what they believed they deserved in life)?

Learning How You Influence Your Self-Esteem

In order to become aware of how you influence your own self-esteem, it is necessary to notice when you engage in thoughts, feelings, or actions that harm or help your self-esteem. In order to work on this awareness, choose any element of the self-esteem system (like treating yourself with respect or loving yourself), take a small notebook with you through the day, and write down whatever you notice in your thoughts, feelings, or actions that is relevant to the element you are observing.

In the evening, review your notes, and add what you have observed to what you know about yourself. Consider whether what you have observed is really how you want to be or how you want to treat yourself. When you are ready, make a commitment to change something specific (e.g., respecting yourself), and write down what you are going to do (e.g., Every time I feel put in an inferior position, I will say to myself, "This isn't right-I deserve equal treatment and an equal share. When I feel confident in this perception, I will start saying this out loud..")

It is especially important to record every time you criticize, demean, punish, or harm yourself, and the reason that you did it. When you review your notes, ask yourself whether these behaviors were necessary and appropriate. Ask yourself what you were trying to accomplish by treating yourself that way. Ask yourself whether you would treat a friend or loved one that way. Think of how you would rather have treated yourself, and imagine doing just that. Then when you catch yourself harming yourself the next day, substitute these more loving and accepting responses.

These self-observations are not a reason to criticize or demean yourself. Everything you learn about yourself can help you to do better. Knowing the truth about yourself allows you to do the most to improve, and it also makes you more independent of the unfair or incorrect observations that others make of you.

Trying Out Elements of the Self-Esteem System

Choose an element from the self-esteem system (e.g., accepting yourself) and every 15 minutes throughout the day ask yourself whether you are using that element of the system, and what it would be like to use it (e.g., ask yourself whether you are accepting yourself at this moment, and what it would be like and what it would require in order to accept yourself at this moment). This is also a good way to discover your resistances to better self-esteem.

Imaging Your Goals

Sit down and relax somewhere where it is quiet and there are no distractions. Close your eyes and concentrate. Allow adequate time—perhaps five to fifteen minutes at a time. Work in the medium that works best for you—that is, if you imagine things in pictures, then do this imaging visually, but if you imagine things best as sounds or feelings, then use those methods.

Imagine yourself in your daily life—being at work, doing the housework, talking to friends, going to meetings or church. As you imagine these activities be aware of how you feel in response to yourself. Now, imagine what it would be like to be doing those same activities with positive self-esteem. Let yourself enjoy the difference.

Include in your imaging all the various evidences of self-esteem from Part I—Chapter Two. Take each of these aspects in turn and imagine yourself feeling or doing it. For example, imagine respecting yourself, how it would feel, in what situations you would like to feel it, and how you would act and feel if you did respect yourself. Imagine saying to yourself, "I respect myself, and it feels good," or "I accept myself for who I am, and it feels good." Imaging the whole list of evidences of self-esteem will take several sessions. You can stop when you are tired, but come back to it until you have created a set of images that cover all aspects of the positive self-esteem that you want to feel. You can use these images on a daily basis, to remind yourself of what you want to achieve.

If you like structure, write out or make a chart of each of the elements of self-esteem, together with the key situations relevant to each in your life and the new responses you wish to cultivate.

Daily Self-Esteem Affirmation

Start every day with images of the positive self-esteem behaviors you wish for yourself for that day, even before you get out of bed. First read the Daily Self-Esteem Meditation and Affirmation in Part V--Resource 2, and then imagine how you will implement the affirmation in your actual behavior that day. Make a copy of the affirmation so you can carry it with you and read it for support during the day. Carry a small notebook with you so that you can jot down how you criticize yourself, etc., so that you can consider these things each evening.

General Self-Esteem Affirmations and Intentions

In addition to using the Daily Self-Esteem Meditation and Affirmation in Part V--Resource 2, set aside some time each day to use the Self-Esteem Affirmations and Intentions in Part V--Resource 4. As you say each one to yourself, let yourself imagine acting it out in your daily life.

Establishing New Self-Perceptions and Attitudes

Choose an element from the system (e.g., respecting yourself). At least three times a day, practice expressing this perception or attitude to yourself, using images from the imaging you did in the exercise above. In front of a mirror, tell yourself the new perception or attitude (e.g., say to yourself "I respect you; you are a fine person, and you deserve basic respect from everyone."). Say this several times. Notice how it feels. Do your best to let it feel good and to appreciate yourself for doing something good for yourself. Act out the behaviors you have planned in your imaging. Appreciate yourself for trying to treat yourself better.

Do One Nice Thing For Yourself Every Day

Every day, do at least one nice or good thing for yourself. At first, it will help to decide the night before what you will do. Later, you will be able to recognize opportunities spontaneously as they occur.

Obviously doing nice things for yourself should feel good, but at first it may bring out all the conflicts you have about whether you deserve good things, whether your love for yourself is worth anything, whether you deserve an equal share, etc., etc. Notice these hesitancies and conflicts and think them through until you understand where they are coming from and how they are stopping you from treating yourself better.

Carry out your plan for doing these nice things for yourself, despite the conflicts you may feel. This will help you learn even more about your conflicts (and you will get the benefit of treating yourself well).

Practice Accepting Yourself

Accepting yourself and loving yourself are so important that they deserve their own practice exercises. Practice accepting yourself. Say to yourself "I really am acceptable, and I accept myself." Say it over a few times out loud to yourself. Say it to yourself in the mirror. See how it feels. "I really am acceptable, and I accept myself." It feels good, though it may feel unusual and may be something you will need to get used to. Enjoy the feeling. Practice allowing yourself to be yourself. Learn how to be without worrying about yourself or questioning yourself.

Practice Loving Yourself

Check out whether you treat yourself in a loving way. On a chosen day, from the moment you wake to the time you go to sleep, ask yourself every fifteen minutes how it would be to respond to yourself at that moment in a loving way. When you ask yourself that question, look at what you are doing and imagine what a loving observer would do or say. Then imagine doing or saying that loving thing to yourself, and see what it would feel like.

Express your love for yourself to yourself. Say to yourself (in the mirror if possible), "I love you; you are a wonderful person, and you deserve love. I want the best for you, and I'll do everything I can to make your life good."

In addition, do one thing each day that expresses that love for yourself. Do it regardless of your resistance or embarrassment.

Looking Forward

This completes our exploration of self-esteem. You now have the tools to make your self-esteem positive and to maintain it that way, and this will allow you to relish every day as a new opportunity for enjoyment and accomplishment. You will still have the same practical problems that we all face, but you will face them with a positive attitude and without blaming yourself for things that are not your fault or for things that are realistically beyond your control.

If you feel able to do so, spread the word about self-esteem to others. Copy the "Abbreviated Self-Esteem Bill of Rights and Duties" from Part V--Resource 3 of the book and put it up on bulletin boards. Use it in classrooms to help children understand self-esteem and as a guide to getting along better. Expose the inappropriate behavior of others when they use put-downs in order to gain advantage. Stand up for your self-esteem rights openly, and say clearly what you are doing, by quoting from this book. Form self-esteem support groups and use this book as a study guide. Join local organizations that exist to promote the self-esteem cause, such as your local task force on self-esteem, or the National Council on Self-Esteem. (See Part V -Resource 5 for some names and addresses.) Seek friends who are sympathetic to everyone's need for self-esteem and who want to make good self-esteem possible for others.

The ideas in this book have been apparent to insightful people for thousands of years, even though all of them are not emphasized in the current, "feel good" self-help literature. I hope that by explaining and reinforcing these ideas, this book has given you more confidence in your basic worth and more determination to stand up for your self-esteem rights. My very best wishes on your journey to better self-esteem!

PART FIVE

VALUABLE RESOURCES

Resource 1

EVALUATING YOUR OWN SELF-ESTEEM

Christopher Ebbe, Ph.D. © 1987

The following items and questions will help you understand better the feelings you have toward yourself and help you get an idea of the level of your self-esteem. Every person has some positive and some negative feelings about himself or herself, and you will have a chance here to express and recognize some of those feelings. Be as honest as you can be, since that will give you the most information about yourself. Some of your feelings and thoughts may surprise you, but try not to hide them from yourself or pretend that you feel differently than you really do.

Name_____

Age_____ Sex_____

Educational Level_____
Vocation/Job_____

Ethnic/Cultural Background_____

For the following questions, check the response that fits you best.

1. How do you feel about yourself most of the time?
   _____ very good
   _____ good
   _____ neutral
   _____ bad
   _____ very bad

2. How valuable do you feel inside yourself as a person, separate

from how others feel about you?
_____ worthless
_____ not worth much
_____ some value
_____ valuable
_____ very valuable

3. How much respect do you have for yourself?
_____ a lot
_____ quite a bit
_____ a medium amount
_____ a little
_____ none

4. To what degree do you accept yourself?
_____ not at all
_____ a little
_____ a medium amount
_____ quite a bit
_____ a lot

5. How much do you like yourself?
_____ a lot
_____ quite a bit
_____ a medium amount
_____ a little
_____ not at all

6. How much do you love yourself?
_____ not at all
_____ a little
_____ a medium amount
_____ quite a bit
_____ a lot

7. How much enjoyment do you get just from being yourself?
   ____ none
   ____ a little
   ____ a medium amount
   ____ quite a bit
   ____ a lot

8. How satisfied are you with yourself?
   ____ quite satisfied
   ____ moderately satisfied
   ____ in between
   ____ moderately dissatisfied
   ____ quite dissatisfied

9. How much of the time do you think of yourself as an equal of those around you?
   ____ almost all the time
   ____ often
   ____ half the time
   ____ seldom
   ____ almost never

10. How much right do you think you have to really be yourself?
    ____ none
    ____ a little
    ____ a medium amount
    ____ quite a bit
    ____ a lot

11. How free do you feel to have your own opinions and feelings about things?
    ____ completely free
    ____ fairly free
    ____ somewhat free
    ____ not very free
    ____ not free at all

12. How much of the time do you act in accordance with what you feel and believe inside (as opposed to what you think others want from you)?

_____ almost never
_____ seldom
_____ half the time
_____ often
_____ almost all the time

13. TRUE ___ FALSE ___ Quite often I pretend to think or feel like others do in order to keep them happy with me.

14. How much right do you think you have to exist and to be a part of the world?

_____ none
_____ a little
_____ a medium amount
_____ quite a bit
_____ total right

15. TRUE ___ FALSE ___ Often I feel guilty just for being alive.

16. TRUE ___ FALSE ___ Sometimes I feel I am supposed to be dead or not be around any more.

17. How much do you deserve in life?

_____ an equal share with other people
_____ somewhat less than other people
_____ half as much as other people
_____ a lot less than other people
_____ almost nothing

18. To what degree do you believe that there is something about you or something wrong with you that causes others to treat you badly?

_____ strongly believe this
_____ generally believe this
_____ a medium amount
_____ generally don't believe this

_____ don't believe this at all

If you do believe this, what is it that's wrong with you?

19. How important are your needs, compared to those of others?
_____ my needs are just as important as others' needs
_____ somewhat less important than others' needs
_____ half as important as others' needs
_____ a lot less important than others' needs
_____ almost totally unimportant

20. How much does your feeling good about yourself depend on things that prove how much you are worth (like having nice possessions, being pretty, getting awards, having a lot of money, being married, being "better than" other people, etc.)?
_____ almost completely depends on these things
_____ quite a bit
_____ a medium amount
_____ a little bit
_____ does not depend on these things at all

21. How much do you expect of yourself?
_____ I expect perfection
_____ I expect far more than what is reasonable and appropriate
_____ I expect somewhat more than what is reasonable and appropriate
_____ I expect a little more than what is reasonable and appropriate.
_____ I expect what is reasonable and appropriate

22. To what degree are you harsh and punitive with yourself when you evaluate and judge yourself and your behavior (like calling yourself names, criticizing yourself, punishing yourself, etc.)?
_____ very harsh and punitive
_____ quite harsh and punitive
_____ a medium amount
_____ a little bit harsh and punitive
_____ not harsh and punitive

23. How often do you automatically feel bad about yourself when someone else is upset with you or isn't getting what he or she wants from you?

_____ almost all the time

_____ often

_____ half the time

_____ seldom

_____ almost never

24. How adequate do you think you are in meeting the demands of life?

_____ quite inadequate

_____ somewhat inadequate

_____ somewhere in the middle

_____ somewhat adequate

_____ quite adequate

25. To what degree do you see yourself as a success in life?

_____ very much a success

_____ quite a bit of a success

_____ a medium amount

_____ a partial failure

_____ almost a total failure

26. How well do you meet your own needs?

_____ quite well

_____ reasonably well

_____ a medium amount

_____ not very well

_____ poorly

27. How much confidence do you have in yourself?

_____ none

_____ a little

_____ a medium amount

_____ quite a bit

_____ a lot

28. How much of the time are you trustworthy and responsible toward yourself (able to trust yourself to do what is right for you)?

____ almost all the time
____ often
____ half the time
____ seldom
____ almost never

29. How often do you comfort and support yourself when you need it?

____ almost never
____ seldom
____ half the time
____ often
____ almost all the time

30. How often do you do nice things for yourself—things that are good for you or pleasurable for you?

____ almost all the time
____ often
____ half the time
____ seldom
____ almost never

31. How often do you do what will really be best for you?

____ almost never
____ seldom
____ half the time
____ often
____ almost all the time

32. How often do you criticize and blame yourself?

____ almost all the time
____ often
____ half the time
____ seldom
____ almost never

33. How comfortable are you being with other people in general?
____ quite comfortable
____ moderately comfortable
____ in between
____ moderately uncomfortable
____ quite uncomfortable

34. How much of the time do you expect to get esteem, respect, and acceptance from other people?
____ almost all the time
____ often
____ half the time
____ seldom
____ almost never

35. How much of the time do you think you are enough to keep others interested and satisfied?
____ almost all the time
____ often
____ half the time
____ seldom
____ almost never

36. How much of the time do you insist on respect and equal treatment from others?
____ almost never
____ seldom
____ half the time
____ often
____ almost all the time

37. Are you assertive in trying to get what you need from others, or do you pretty much wait and take what they are willing to give?
____ very assertive
____ quite assertive
____ partly assertive, partly not
____ mostly unassertive
____ completely unassertive

38. How do you respond when people you know treat you badly, abuse you, or put you down?

_____ I insist that they stop, and if they don't, I refuse to be around them.

_____ I let them know that it's not right, and sometimes I stop being around them.

_____ I may protest, but I probably won't stop relating to them.

_____ I rarely say anything, and I continue to relate to them.

_____ I never say anything, and I continue to relate to them.

39. How do you respond when people put you down inappropriately for who you are (like for your race or religion or your social status)?

_____ I just take it, without making any protest.

_____ Occasionally I say I don't like it.

_____ Half the time I protest or complain.

_____ Most of the time I protest or complain.

_____ I always protest or complain.

HOW TO USE YOUR SELF-EVALUATION

The multiple choice items can be interpreted simply by looking at the overall picture communicated by your answers. They can also be scored by finding the scores on the following pages for the answers you gave and adding them up. The first score listed is for the first option on that question, the second for the second option, etc. (Note that the TRUE/FALSE items are not scored.)

Scores can range from 180 to 36. This score should be taken only as a very general indicator of self-esteem level (since it has not been validated through research). Assuming that the questions were answered truthfully and candidly, it would be fair to say that a person with a score of 180 would have a high level of self-esteem, while a person with a score of 36 would have very low self-esteem.

1-5	2-1	3-5	4-1	5-5	6-1	7-1	8-5	9-5	10-1	11-5
4	2	4	2	4	2	2	4	4	2	4
3	3	3	3	3	3	3	3	3	3	3
2	4	2	4	2	4	4	2	2	4	2
1	5	1	5	1	5	5	1	1	5	1

12-1	14-1	17-5	18-1	19-5	20-1	21-1	22-1	23-1
2	2	4	2	4	2	2	2	2
3	3	3	3	3	3	3	3	3
4	4	2	4	2	4	4	4	4
5	5	1	5	1	5	5	5	5

24-1	25-5	26-5	27-1	28-5	29-1	30-5	31-1	32-1
2	4	4	2	4	2	4	2	2
3	3	3	3	3	3	3	3	3
4	2	2	4	2	4	2	4	4
5	1	1	5	1	5	1	5	5

33-5	34-5	35-5	36-1	37-5	38-5	39-1
4	4	4	2	4	4	2
3	3	3	3	3	3	3
2	2	2	4	2	2	4
1	1	1	5	1	1	5

DAILY SELF-ESTEEM MEDITATION AND AFFIRMATION

Christopher Ebbe, Ph.D. (1986)

Read and meditate on the following statements every morning when you arise. Reflect on them throughout your day.

I want to feel good about myself and to respect, accept, and love myself, and I commit myself again to do all that I must do in order to have these feelings.

I want to know myself better, and I will let myself be aware of all my thoughts, needs, and feelings, so that I can manage my life better. All of my thoughts, needs, and feelings are a part of me, and I can lovingly and with compassion accept them all.

I will be honest with myself about myself and about others and will not try to make myself or anyone else look any better or any worse than they actually are. I will notice how my behavior affects other people and will consider whether this is how I want to affect them. I will let others have their individual reactions to me, knowing that their reactions sometimes have little to do with me and do not by themselves make me good or bad, anyway. I know that there is a reason why I do each thing that I do, and I will acknowledge honestly my desires and motives to myself, in order to understand myself better.

I am moving toward having healthier and more positive attitudes, beliefs, and assumptions about myself. I believe that I have a perfect right to exist and to be in this world, and I grant that right to everyone else as well. I believe that I have the right to be myself, with all my thoughts, needs, and feelings, and I am coming to be more comfortable with who I am.

I believe that as a person I am fundamentally equal to everyone else, and I will not accept any attempts to define me as inferior. As an equal I have just as much right as anyone else to good things in life, as well as complete freedom to decide what I want in life and to pursue it. I approach other people positively, expecting as their equal to have their esteem, respect, and acceptance in most circumstances, but allowing them the right not to relate if that is their preference.

I am cultivating positive feelings toward myself, and I will practice having these feelings for myself today. I respect myself and treat myself in a self-respecting manner. I accept myself as I am, with all my thoughts, needs, and feelings, and I refuse to criticize or reject myself, even though there may be some things about me that I want to change. I know that accepting myself is the best way to help myself feel good about me. I like myself, and I enjoy my own company. As I learn to do more and more good things for myself, I like myself even more. I love myself and will treat myself lovingly and with compassion. I enjoy being me, and I am enjoying being myself more each day. I am satisfied with myself and with where I am in life right now. I have hopes and dreams for the future, but today I am satisfied with myself for who I am right now.

I do not judge myself harshly any longer but view myself reasonably and with compassion. I question all standards and expectations that I have for myself and that others have for me, because I believe that in the end the only things that matter are the impact my behavior has on myself and on others. I refuse to be controlled by the expectations and reactions of others, and I no longer feel bad about myself if I choose not to do what others want me to do. I keep my conscience clear by doing the best I can and by forgiving myself as appropriate.

Because I love myself and want the best for myself, I take my needs seriously and treat myself well. I enjoy taking good care of myself and doing nice things for myself. I have come to trust myself to take good care of me by always being trustworthy and responsible toward myself.

Above all, I want to be more myself every day, experiencing all that there is, learning all that I can, enjoying the company of others, and expressing myself as lovingly, assertively, and creatively as possible.

Resource 3

AN ABBREVIATED SELF-ESTEEM BILL OF RIGHTS AND DUTIES

Christopher Ebbe, Ph.D., ABPP
(1986, 2003)

This bill of rights and duties summarizes self-esteem rights that everyone should have, as well as some responsibilities that we each have if we wish to have good self-esteem.

1. Every person has the right to have good self-esteem and to feel good about himself.
2. Every child has a right to the love, nurturance, respect, and acceptance that are necessary for the development of healthy self-esteem.
3. Every person has the right to feel lovable and to love herself.
4. Every person has the right to seek and to feel pleasure and joy.
5. Every person has the right to basic respect from others at all times.
6. Every person is basically the equal of others and has the right to be treated by others fundamentally as an equal.
7. Every person has the right to have the same things expected or asked of her as are expected of others in the same group.
8. Every person has the right to be accepted by others as a person and to have his expressions, desires, and behaviors accepted, as long as they are not harming others.
9. Every person has the duty to take charge of and to be the primary determiner of her self-esteem.
10. Every person is at all times in charge of and responsible for her behavior and her feelings.
11. Every person has the right to complete awareness of his own thoughts, feelings, needs, desires, motives, and potentials.

12. Every person has the right to have opinions of self and feeling reactions to self independent of the feelings, reactions, expectations, and standards of others for her, and every person has the right to build an autonomous sense of self and identity, independent of the desires and needs of parents, other people, or the group.
13. Every person has the right to establish reasonable and humane standards for self, as long as those standards do not directly threaten group security.
14. Every person has the right to see the truth about himself, others, society, and the world, and the right to freedom and choice in beliefs and in ways of understanding the world.
15. Every person has the right and every person who wants to have good self-esteem has the duty to take steps to ensure that she is treated well by others, including insisting on being appropriately respected and accepted by others and insisting on being treated by others as an essential equal.
16. Every person has the right to terminate relationships in which the other person will not and cannot be induced to treat one according to principles and conditions essential to healthy self-esteem, including respect and acceptance, honoring one's rights, not abusing or taking advantage of one, and not placing one in an inferior role or status. Every person also has the right to seek relationships in which these conditions are met.
17. No person is obligated to feel bad or to restrict his actions so that someone else can feel better.

Resource 4

SELF-ESTEEM AFFIRMATIONS AND INTENTIONS

Christopher Ebbe, Ph.D.

The statements below can be used throughout the day to affirm to yourself your beliefs, values, and intentions regarding your self-esteem. Copy these pages and carry the copy with you so that you can take time mid-morning, at lunchtime, and mid-afternoon to review them. Say them out loud if your environment permits.

1. It is a good thing to be aware of all of my thoughts, feelings, needs, and motives. I will let myself be aware of everything within me at all times, without shame or conflict.
2. My basic value as a person is not determined by the reactions of others to me. My basic worth and value as a person are within me and cannot be destroyed by others.
3. I will be completely honest with myself about myself and other people, since I am willing to know the truth about myself and others, even if it is not to my liking.
4. I am in charge of how I view and understand myself, and I am the chief determiner of my self-esteem. The views and feelings of others are their own limited and often self-serving reactions and do not by themselves determine my self-esteem. I take responsibility for doing what is needed to feel good about myself.
5. I value myself and others for what matters-how we behave and how we impact the lives of others-rather than for superficial values such as appearance, wealth, possessions, and social status.
6. I am willing to change, and I am willing to perceive myself as worthwhile and valuable. I am committed to treating myself well and to building a nurturing and positive relationship with

myself.

7. There is much that is right about me, and there is nothing wrong with me. Nothing about me causes others to mistreat me or to view me as inferior, and nothing about me justifies others in mistreating me or in viewing me as inferior.

8. I have a perfect right to exist and to be myself in this world. I am fundamentally the equal of others and deserve fair and equal treatment from everyone at all times. My needs are as important as the needs of others, and I have the same right as others to the good things in life that are available to all.

9. I am OK just as I am, and I am satisfied with myself just the way I am right now, even though there may be things that I still wish to change about myself.

10. I can relax about being myself, since I am OK the way I am, and there is nothing about me that must be criticized or changed.

11. I am enough to keep others satisfied in healthy and mutually nurturing relationships.

12. I respect myself and treat myself with respect.

13. I accept myself completely, just as I am, even though there may be things that I still wish to change about myself.

14. I love myself, and it feels great! The more good things I do for myself, the more I love myself.

15. I enjoy being with myself and being aware of all of the wonderful things about myself.

16. I have stopped trying to control my behavior by judging myself harshly and punitively. Instead, I try at all times to do what will be truly best for myself.

17. I decide for myself whether I have done something wrong, instead of automatically feeling bad whenever someone else is upset with me.

18. I set my own reasonable and humane standards for myself, and I do not allow others to impose unreasonable and inappropriate expectations and standards on me.

19. I try my best to live by my chosen values and standards, so I can avoid feeling shame and guilt and so that I can be an example of integrity for others.

20. I treat myself well, including meeting my needs acceptably, being responsible and trustworthy toward myself, doing what will truly be best for me, treating myself in a loving and

compassionate way, comforting myself when I need it, taking good care of myself, and being kind to myself. I have stopped criticizing and blaming myself inappropriately.

21. In order to create good relationships with others, I am learning to have accurate and caring empathy with others and to understand their needs. I am becoming more comfortable being around others, since I am equal and not inferior to them. I am learning to be appropriately assertive in asking for what I need from others.

22. I deserve basic respect from others at all times. I deserve basic acceptance from others as long as my behavior is not harming them inappropriately.

23. I try hard to make sure that others treat me in ways that do not tear down my self-esteem. I insist on basic respect from others, and I insist on being treated as fundamentally the equal of others. I do not tolerate mistreatment or being put-down by others, and I tell others how I wish to be treated. If others are not willing to treat me appropriately, I withdraw from them and seek other, more supportive, affirming, and gratifying relationships. I speak up in opposition to attitudes and behaviors that unfairly define certain people as inferior and undeserving.

24. I seek at all times to be myself with integrity and to express in my life and behavior the things that I believe in.

Resource 5

HOW TO GET INVOLVED IN THE SELF-ESTEEM MOVEMENT

If you would like to get more involved in the self-esteem movement, here is a national organization devoted to the promotion of self-esteem. It's quarterly newsletter, "Self-Esteem Today" ($20 subscription), provides stimulating reading.

National Association for Self-Esteem
P.O. Box 3511
New Hyde Park, NY 11040
(516) 621-0878

APPENDIX

BIBLIOGRAPHY ON SELF-ESTEEM AND SELF-FEELINGS

Alberti, Robert & Emmons, Michael. Your Perfect Right. San Luis Obispo: Impact, 1975.

Andrews, Lewis. To Thine Own Self Be True. Garden City, N.J.: Anchor Press, 1987.

Barksdale, Lilburn S. Building Self-Esteem. Idyllwild, CA: The Barksdale Foundation, 1972.

Barksdale, Lilburn S. Essays on Self-Esteem. Idyllwild, CA: The Barksdale Foundation, 1977.

Bernhard, Yetta. Self-Care. Millbrae CA: Celestial Arts, 1975.

Borba, Michelle & Borba, Craig. Self-Esteem: A Classroom Affair— 101 Ways To Help Children Like Themselves. San Francisco: Harper and Row, 1978.

Branden, Nathaniel. Honoring The Self. Los Angeles: Jeremy Tarcher, 1983.

Branden, Nathaniel. How To Raise Your Self-Esteem. New York: Bantam, 1987.

Branden, Nathaniel. The Power of Self-Esteem. Deerfield Beach FL: Health Communications, 1992.

Branden, Nathaniel. The Psychology of Self-Esteem. New York: Avon Books, 1973.

Briggs, Dorothy Corkille. Celebrate Your Self (Enhancing Your Own Self-Esteem). New York: Doubleday, 1977.

Briggs, Dorothy Corkille. Your Child's Self-Esteem. New York: Doubleday, 1970.

Browne, Harry. How I Found Freedom In An Unfree World. New York: Macmillan, 1973.

California Task Force To Promote Self-esteem and Personal and Social Responsibility. Toward A State Of Esteem. Sacramento CA: State Dep't. of Education, 1990.

Canfield, Jack & Wells, Harold. 100 Ways To Enhance Self-concept In the Classroom. Englewood Cliffs, N.J.: Prentice-Hall, 1976.

Collins, Vincent. Me, Myself, & You. St. Meinrad, Ind.: Abbey Press, 1976.

Dobson, James. Hide Or Seek. Old Tappan, N.J.: Fleming H. Revell Co., 1979.

Ellsworth, Barry. Living In Love With Yourself. Salt Lake City: Breakthrough, 1988.

Frey, Diane & Carlock, C. Jesse. Enhancing Self Esteem. Muncie, Ind.: Accelerated Development, 1984. Gardner, M. Robert. Self Inquiry. Boston: Little Brown, 1983.

Gendlin, Eugene. Focusing. New York: Bantam Books, 1981.

Harmon, Ed & Jarmin, Marge. Taking Charge of My Life. Idylwild CA: Barksdale Foundation, 1988.

Harrill, Suzanne. You Could Feel Good. Houston: Innerworks, 1987.

Harris, Sydney. The Authentic Person. Niles, Ill.: Argus, 1972.

Harris, Thomas. I'm O.K.—You're O.K. New York: Avon, 1969.

Hendricks, Gay. Learning To Love Yourself. New York: Prentice-Hall, 1982.

Jampolsky, Gerald. Teach Only Love. New York: Bantam, 1983.

Kaufman, Barry. To Love Is To Be Happy With. New York: Fawcett, 1977.

Keyes, Ken. Handbook To Higher Consciousness. St. Mary, Ky.: Cornucopia Institute, 1975.

Khalsa, SiriNam. Group Exercises for Enhancing Social Skills & Self-Esteem. Sarasota FL: Professional Resources Press, 1996.

Lair, Jess. I Ain't Much, Baby—But I'm All I've Got. New York: Fawcett, 1972.

Mack, John & Ablon, Steven (eds.). The Development and Sustaining of Self-Esteem In Childhood. New York: Int'l. Univ's. Press, 1983.

Mandel, Bob. Open Heart Therapy. Berkeley: Celestial Arts, 1984.

McKay, Matthew & Fanning, Patrick. Self-Esteem. Oakland, CA: New Harbinger Pub's., 1987.

Michael, Andrew. A Road Map To An Esteeming Workplace. (draft copy), 1991.

Phelps, Stanlee & Austin, Nancy. The Assertive Woman. San Luis Obispo, CA: Impact, 1975.

Pollard, John. Self-Parenting: The Complete Guide to Your Inner Conversations. Malibu CA: Generic Human Studies Publications, 1987.

Pope, Alice; McHale, Susan; & Craighead, W. Edward. Self-Esteem Enhancement With Children and Adolescents. New York: Pergamon, 1988.

Porat, Frieda. Positive Selfishness. Millbrae, CA: Celestial Arts, 1977.

Ray, Sondra. I Deserve Love. Millbrae, CA: Les Femmes, 1976.

Ray, Sondra. Loving Relationships. Millbrae, CA: Celestial Arts, 1980.

Ridley, Matt. The Origins of Virtue: Human Instincts and the Evolution of Cooperation.Viking, 1997. [argues that positive human interactions are more adaptive than negative ones]

Rusk, Tom & Read, Randy. I Want To Change, But I Don't Know How. San Diego: Blue Pacific Books, 1978.

Sanford, Linda & Donovan, Mary Ellen. Women and Self-Esteem. New York: Viking Penguin, 1984.

Schuller, Robert. Self-Love. New York: Pillar Books, 1969.

Semigran, Candace. One-Minute Self-Esteem—Caring for Yourself and Others. New York: Bantam, 1988.

Smith, Manuel. When I Say No, I Feel Guilty. New York: Bantam, 1975.

Wegscheider-Cruse, Sharon. Learning To Love Yourself. Deerfield Beach FL: Health Communications, 1987.